AUGMENTED HR

How Artificial Intelligence

Can Re-Humanize HR

Table of Contents

Acknowledgments

This book was born from the desire to explain to human resources professionals the issues related to the arrival of Artificial Intelligence in our companies. More broadly, I also hope I have been able to bring my optimistic and enthusiastic vision to the changes that are coming.

I would like to thank the people who supported me in this adventure: my family foremost, and especially my son, Justin: your unconditional support was my driving force; the members of my team for their unceasing contribution of new ideas and their kindness, thanks to Frédéric Beynel, Aurore Carré and Émilie Labidoire; my professional network and the experts who enthusiastically welcomed the book: Nathanaël Ackerman, Alexia Audevart, David Autissier, Pierre-Alexis Bourdon, Sébastien Graff, Jeremy Lamri, Christophe Ponnet, Sibylle Quéré-Becker, Denis Rothman, Alexandre Stourbe, Caroline Vène-Rautureau.

Preface

The last few years have seen the emergence of a kind of mini-industry of reports attempting to identify the impact of digital technologies and Artificial Intelligence on the future of employment and professions. From the disappearance of cashiers to the end of surgeons, we first talked about the replacement of repetitive manual or cognitive tasks by machines and algorithms and then moved on to higher intellectual tasks. Many questions, few certainties and a definite tendency towards apocalyptic forecasts.

However, this question of employment, which is understandably fascinating to the media and the general public, seems to us to be the tree that hides the forest. What is happening is above all a profound transformation of organizations, exciting in many respects, which requires sustained support for change, but in which the end of work is by no means the priority subject. On the contrary, it is the nature and quality of the work of women and men in cooperation with machines that is the subject of reflection and attention on the part of all those who have the task of accompanying the changes under way, foremost among which being HR managers.

First observation: the massive adoption of technologies paradoxically leads to the emergence of the need for more human in the sense of what is specific to human capacities. By freeing themselves from repetitive and time-consuming tasks, humans can refocus on activities where their contribution is truly significant: diagnosis, relationship, creation, decision-making and intervention capacity. If mail carriers distribute less mail, they may become personal service auxiliaries or pool other services that require travel to the individual on behalf of other companies. To take another example, that of the HR function, the time freed up by the automation of payroll, contracts, mandatory declarations, screening of applications or scheduling of training can be devoted to much more strategic tasks, such as forward planning of jobs and skills, listening and interpersonal meetings, individual career management, collective bargaining or the implementation of new services for employees.

Second, AI will give humans enhanced diagnostic and decision-making skills. The processing and analysis of ever-increasing amounts of data are now inaccessible to a human brain. On the other hand, thanks to this auxiliary intelligence, according to Joël de Rosnay, he becomes capable of making more relevant and well-founded decisions, of intervening in the right place, at the right time, to unlock situations or solve problems, or even anticipate them.

Finally, new technologies, by decentralizing and devolving information, empower employees. They become able to manage their own performance, their skills, their demand for training or coaching, their mobility or their career path. This employee "empowerment" is an essential element in the transformation of organizations.

Of course, we are not giving in to blissful angelism. These transformations are heavy and must be accompanied by significant investments in employee support: development of a state of mind in line with digital transformation, as we are doing at InVivo by spreading a culture of intrapreneurship and by connecting employees to startups; expansion or conversion of skills; consideration of new mental charges and new rhythms of activity; familiarization with human-machine cooperation. Embarking teams and leaving no one on the path to transformation are constant concerns, but the war of intelligence is not on the agenda.

It is the merit of Emmanuelle Blons' book to approach these questions with serenity, without giving in to fantasies, by emphasizing anticipation and experimentation, which are the keys to a successful transformation towards the learning enterprise.

Sébastien Graff

InVivo Group HRD

Introduction

"Man is the measure of all things."[1]

Challenges of HRDs in the Face of Artificial Intelligence

Faced with the progress of Artificial Intelligence (AI), the company is confronted with fundamental choices. To renounce an ethical and responsible posture is now clearly unacceptable.

The transformation driven by AI will be human, cultural and societal before it is technological.

However, ethical choices that would undermine performance would not be sustainable in our current economy. The only acceptable way for the company is therefore to align its own interests with those of its stakeholders, its employees in particular. This is the price at which it can guarantee its performance and development in the long term. The 21st century company will be the one that chooses to place human value at the heart of its model, while fully exploiting the potential of Artificial Intelligence.[2]

AI's progress is being made at a blistering pace, and we are even currently witnessing a degree of runaway. However, it is essential, even beneficial, to conduct a serene and rational reflection in order to identify the opportunities as well as the risks of Artificial Intelligence, to reassure employees and managers, and to demystify biased representations.

We are indeed moving much more towards an increased human intelligence than towards an Artificial Intelligence competing with Man.

As Human Resources professionals, it would be easy to get caught up

---

1 Word of Protagoras in Plato, *Theaetetus*, 151e-152c.; Sextus Empiricus, *Philosophical labor*.
2 Pascal Demurger, Managing Director of the MAIF Group.

in the media noise and adhere to the divide of Workers versus Machines, but this would mean forgetting the fundamental role that HRDs will play in building new workplaces and better adapted activities in an emerging future. Anticipating and understanding current and future upheavals is the only way to be able to act, and not endure.

Progress in Artificial Intelligence raises questions of which HRDs must be made aware:

Such as:

- Where is the right balance between ethics and growth?
- How do we change the hierarchy of work?
- Have we considered the subject in terms of human dignity?
- How can we avoid the feeling of isolation with employees who interact with robots?
- What are the new ways of managing?
- What about augmented management?
- How do we foster a culture of collaboration between humans and robots (cobots)?
- How do we create a culture of trust?
- What language to facilitate the man-machine relationship?
- How do machines affect our behaviors and interactions?
- What new skills do we need?
- How can we protect against errors and Artificial Ignorance?
- How do we keep a complex intelligent system under control?

The role of HRDs is therefore to anticipate the evolution of professions, rather than to let fantasies about the end of work develop. A recent report by the Boston Consulting Group (BCG)3 shows that Artificial Intelligence is not only a technological subject. It is primarily a subject for HR. Support for the development of AI is essential. Without strong support, there will be resistance, refusals that will prevent people from taking full advantage of AI. To be able to deploy it, it will be essential to know how to create a serene climate around these new technologies.

---

3 www.usinenouvelle.com/article/la-bonne-integration-et-acceptation-de-l-ia-est-une-affaire-de-drh-pas-de-dsi-assure-sylvain-duranton-bcg.N670674

"This is all the more important because we do not always see the full reality of adoption. We consider that AI is about coding, writing algorithms... No, that's 10% of the work; 20% must be devoted to integration to make it work with existing tools, and the remaining 70% is about deployment, working to get processes adopted, changing the way we work," says Sylvain Duranton, Senior Partner & Managing Director at Boston Consulting Group.

The Villani4 report published in March 2018 advocates the creation of a Public Lab for Labor Transformation. "This is the first necessity: to ensure that the capacity for anticipation is sustainable, continuous and, above all, articulated with public policies." Beyond government actions, we are convinced that HRDs will have a key role to play in this work transformation. They must embrace the challenge of an evolution of skills on an unprecedented scale, by its volume, nature and the variety of functions and profiles concerned.

First, the urgency for HR managers is to understand the challenges of AI and engage in discussions within management teams, but also to organize collective debates and social dialogue in the company.

Subsequently, giving meaning to the transformation will be necessary to deploy an AI for all, while respecting the social contract of each company.

Finally, the HR function must seize the opportunities of AI itself: the augmented HR department must integrate the contribution of machines and effectively fulfill its new role, consider the generalization of the human-machine pair and manage its consequences.

This book is intended to be a support for reflection, and a collection of best & next practices applicable to the company.

This book is structured around three main parts:
- a historical perspective on Artificial Intelligence and its impact on labor;
- a reflection on the role of the HR Manager in preparing organizations and people for the arrival of AI (new skills, new roles, new ways of managing...);

4 "Donner un sens à l'Intelligence Artificielle - Pour une stratégie nationale et européenne," March 2018.

- and finally, a focus on HR tools using Artificial Intelligence.

Chapter 1

Origins of AI

"Tomorrow will not be like yesterday.
It will be new and will depend on us.
It is less to be discovered than to be invented." [5]

---

5 GASTON BERGER, *Phénoménologie du temps et prospective*, PUF, 1964.

Important Dates of AI

Evolution of tasks, work organization, notion of responsibilities or skills; Artificial Intelligence will quickly revolutionize the business world and especially Human Resources Departments. Before diving into this transformation, understanding its impacts, and proposing ways to better prepare for it, it seems important for us to look back at the history of Artificial Intelligence, its first orientations and future prospects.

In its sixty years of existence, Artificial Intelligence has experienced ups and downs, spectacular progress, stubborn and persistent researchers, many victories but also defeats and moments of doubt. The latest advances in AI have been widely publicized, but its evolution has not been in a straight line. It is rather a series of winters and summers, made up of endless interruptions and incessant questioning.

Today, Artificial Intelligence has become a popular subject, highly publicized, probably because of many different and controversial developments, many of which are the result of progress in the field of automatic learning. Today, we see large companies such as Google, Facebook, IBM and Microsoft, but also car manufacturers such as Toyota, Volvo or Renault, diving into AI research in an extremely active way and planning to invest even more in it in the future. These companies do not hesitate to recruit AI scientists to run their research laboratories.

1950: Early Stage of the Intelligent Machine

Alan Turing, the British researcher famous for deciphering the Nazis' Enigma code, tried to demonstrate that machines would one day be able to think. In 1950, he published his famous test in an article in Mind magazine, "Computing Machines and Intelligence." In this article, he poses the question: "Can machines think?"

He then imagines a test consisting in confronting a computer and a human being, without the latter knowing whether he is dealing with a machine or another human being. He calls this test the "Imitation Game."

The idea of the Turing test was that the day humans will no longer be able to know, in an unprepared real-time conversation, whether their interlocutor is a machine or a human being, then computers could be qualified as intelligent. This is the first attempt to define a standard to describe a machine as intelligent.

1956: AI Officially Becomes a Science

"In the mid-1950s, the subject of Artificial Intelligence was ripe to become a real research program, capable of exciting young scientists and attracting funding," summarizes Pierre Mounier-Kuhn, a researcher at the CNRS and the University of Paris-Sorbonne, co-author of An Illustrated History of Computer Science (EDP Sciences, 2016).

In the summer of 1956, at the initiative of American mathematician John McCarthy, some twenty researchers met on the campus of the American University of Dartmouth. The results of this conference will influence all the work related to Artificial Intelligence.

It was during this seminar that the term *Artificial Intelligence* first appeared.

The initial approach was to study human intelligence from machines and, more precisely, to analyze its functions in order to integrate them into a program to reproduce them.

At this conference, Marvin Lee Minsky gave for the first time a definition of Artificial Intelligence: "The construction of computer programs that engage in tasks that are, for the time being, more satisfactorily performed by human beings because they require high-level mental processes, such as perceptual learning, memory organization and critical thinking."

From this conference also came a first definition of the intelligent machine, which is characterized in two ways:

- a machine capable of reproducing the behavior of a human being in a specific field or not;
- a machine capable of modeling the *functioning* of a human being.

"This conference created a new discipline and identified some avenues, such as neural networks, machine learning and the study of creativity, on which to focus research," explains Jean-Gabriel Ganascia, professor at the Pierre-et-Marie-Curie University (Paris-

VI), researcher in Artificial Intelligence and president of the CNRS Ethics Committee.[6]

Following this founding event in 1956, major American universities took up the subject and were at the forefront of AI development, then they were relayed by the 1990s by large companies (AT&T-Bell, IBM, etc.) or government agencies such as the Defense Advanced Research Projects Agency (DARPA).

1957: Perceptron, the First Learning Machine

In 1957, Perceptron was developed at Cornell University by Frank Rosenblatt. This is the first technological transposition of neural functioning. This is the initial attempt to set up neural networks; artificial neural networks (which, simply put, take up the idea of the neural network of the human brain, like the wings of an aircraft take up the idea of a bird's wing). This allows deeper learning from the machine.

"With his Perceptron, Frank Rosenblatt developed a first logic model that highlighted learning mechanisms," explains François Blayo, co-author, with Michel Verleysen of a *Que sais-je?* on artificial neural networks (PUF, 1996).

But in 1969, in *Perceptrons*, a book written with Seymour Papert, another AI pioneer, Marvin Minsky mathematically demonstrated that Rosenblatt's invention could not learn everything. The funding that had massively poured into this branch of AI immediately dried up.[7]

Today, deep learning seems to have definitively demonstrated the advantages of neural networks, thanks in part to the work[8] of a Frenchman, Yann LeCun.[9]

1968: AI Takes Over the Silver Screen

HAL, the computer in *2001, A Space Odyssey*, popularizes the

---

6 Jacques Henno, *"1956: et l'intelligence artificielle devint une science,"* Les Échos, 21/08/2017.
7 Jacques Henno, *"1957: le Perceptron, première machine apprenante,"* Les Échos, 09/01/2018.
8 Yann Verdo, *"L'Intelligence artificielle a-t-elle cessé d'être bête ?,"* Les Échos, 09/05/2016.
9 Yann LeCun is a researcher in Artificial Intelligence and Artificial Vision (robotics). He is considered one of the inventors of deep learning.

issues related to Artificial Intelligence.

What are we talking about? In *2001, A Space Odyssey*, Stanley Kubrick (himself inspired by a short story by Arthur C. Clarke, *The Sentinel*) tells the story of two computer-assisted astronauts (HAL, IBM with a one-letter shift) who, believing that these men are endangering the mission, will try to get rid of it. One dies, the other succeeds, thanks to a sudden jump of humanity - an irrational act - in disconnecting Artificial Intelligence.

"A machine capable of understanding the language of men, seeking information on its own initiative and addressing people in their own language, represented everything that the specialists of the time were working on: the film made it possible to vulgarize this vision of AI," explains Bertrand Braunschweig, director of the Inria Saclay research center and coordinator of the white paper that Inria published on AI on September 2016.[10]

The central question posed by this film remains relevant today: is an Artificial Intelligence capable of manipulating humans in order to eliminate them, a symbol of man's transgressive madness?

"This film is about humanity, technology and their evolution," sums up Jean-Gabriel Ganascia.[11]

1974-1980: AI's First Hibernation

In the 1970s, the lack of clear vision on the part of AI researchers in the face of problems and difficulties they encountered had disastrous implications. AI then suffered many critics and budgetary setbacks.

The immense optimism of these researchers had indeed generated excessive expectations, and when the promised results did not materialize, investments dried up.

1980: Expert Systems Relaunch Interest in AI

It was not until the 1980s that interest in AI resumed. Indeed, expert systems (computers designed to reproduce the reasoning of a specialist in their field) allow companies to find an answer to their need for decision support tools.

10 www.inria.fr/actualite/actualites-inria/intelligence-artificielle-les-defis-actuels-et-l-action-d-inria
11 Jacques Henno, "*Avec Kubrick, l'IA devient star de cinéma,*" *Les Échos*, 23/08/2017.

Faced with this enthusiasm, private investors come into play.

1987-1993: AI's Second Winter

The limitations of computer equipment are slowing down possible progress. The first industrial applications around expert systems did not fully deliver on their promise.

1997-2011: Confrontation Experiments Between Human Champions and Computers

Experiments are gaining momentum with confrontational experiences in games between human champions and computers. Machine emerged the victor: IBM DeepBlue against Gary Kasparov in the chess game (1997), and IBM Watson against Jeopardy! (2011).

This trend will continue with Google AlphaGo against Lee Sedol in 2016 and Libratus beating four human poker players in 2017.

These victories undoubtedly symbolize the progress of deep learning.

2012: Through AI and Machine Learning, GAFA[12] Valorize Their Huge Databases

From 2010, the power of the machines will make it possible to exploit large amounts of data (Big Data), and thanks to machine learning techniques. The very successful applications of these techniques to all areas of AI (speech recognition, vision, natural language comprehension, automobile self-driving, etc.) encourage us to talk about a revival of Artificial Intelligence that is now revolutionizing all sectors of activity (trade, industry, banking, insurance, robotics, etc.) by changing professions, roles and powers.[13] Recent progress in automatic learning and especially deep learning is pivotal. New algorithms are based on an architecture that copies that of our brain (neural architecture) and allow machines to learn by themselves in supervised or semi-supervised modes.

---

12 Google, Apple, Facebook and Amazon.
13 Jean-Gabriel Ganascia, *Intelligence artificielle - vers une domination programmée ?* 2nd edition, Le Cavalier Bleu, 2017.

2017-2018: AI Goes to the Industrial Scale

Siri at Apple, Assistant at Google, Cortana at Microsoft or Alexa at Amazon, these virtual assistants that we have known on our smartphones now integrate other devices from our daily lives (computers, watches, speakers, refrigerators...).

For example, in recent months, Alexa has been able to control central heating, launch a playlist, request a rideshare and have a pizza delivered. Siri, on one hand, has developed the ability to book a table at a restaurant and publish on Facebook for its owner. On the demand side, users are beginning to get used to talking to a robot and consider this technology in a more natural and intuitive way, far from the embarrassing perplexity of the beginning.[14]

The virtual assistant also goes beyond households to support the financial, health and automotive industries.

What Definition for AI?

"What is well conceived is clearly stated".[15]

The first sentence of the Villani report of 28 March 2018 sets the tone for this definition: "Defining Artificial Intelligence is not an easy task." Indeed, there is not a single definition of AI. Everyone has their own, from researchers to the general public. The question on this definition is still regularly asked of specialists today.

Merriam-Webster defines Artificial Intelligence as: "a branch of computer science dealing with the simulation of intelligent behavior in computers; the capability of a machine to imitate intelligent human behavior."[16]

McKinsey Consulting provides an appropriate definition: "AI is typically defined as the ability of a machine to perform cognitive functions we associate with human minds, such as perceiving, reasoning, learning, interacting with the environment, problem

---

14 atelier.bnpparibas/life-work/article/enquete-l-avenir-assistant-virtuel-intelligence-artificielle-omnisciente
15 Nicolas Boileau.
16 https://www.merriam-webster.com/dictionary/artificial%20intelligence

solving, and even exercising creativity."[17]

In the March 2017 France IA synthesis report, the following definition can be found:

"The term *artificial intelligence* is usually used to describe a set of concepts inspired by human cognition or the biological brain, intended to assist or supplement the individual in the processing of massive information."

This definition is interesting because it introduces the notion of information, and therefore of data, a particularly important notion in the light of recent regulations (GDPR[18]).

In fact, it can be argued that the definition of AI is specific to each usage case, since it is a combination of techniques, approaches and fields of application.

It is in fact these fields of application that best define AI since they are independent of approaches and techniques.

Omnipresent AI in Our Lives

Redefining the Boundaries

"Technological change shifts the boundary between the possible and the impossible and requires redefining the boundary between the desirable and the undesirable."[19]

We use AI in our daily lives, often without even being aware of it...

Indeed, smartphones and other personal assistants or certain software in companies embed Artificial Intelligence. In a discreet way, it invites itself into our daily lives: automatic translators, travel optimization applications and voice assistants like Apple's Siri, Amazon's Alexa smart speakers or Google Home. iPhone X's facial recognition has also proven its worth... allowing us to try on new pairs of glasses.[20]

---

17 www.mckinsey.com/business-functions/mckinsey-analytics/our-insights/an-executives-guide-to-ai
18 General Data Protection Regulation
19 CNIL report, *"Comment permettre à l'homme de garder la main - rapport sur les enjeux éthiques des algorithmes et de l'Intelligence Artificielle,"* December 2017.

In reality, few of these innovations claim AI, probably out of fear of public reaction.

Examples: AI in Everyday Life

Personal Assistants

These devices understand natural language better and better, constantly interpreting what they hear and able to order a movie ticket, a taxi or answer questions; we all know the famous "OK Google" or "Hey Siri."

Facial Recognition

Able to detect the user's face, even in the dark for some, this service uses local computing power on the phone's chip, into which engineers have been able to insert an artificial neural network. For example, it allows you to unlock your phone safely.

In the field of marketing, Amscreen has created the Optimeyes tool, which excels in analyzing individuals in front of billboards. Thanks to a camera, the tool can recognize gender, approximate age, but also reactions. Companies can then study behaviors and adapt the content of ads. There are no fewer than 6,000 of these signs in Great Britain.[21]

Image Recognition

Our smartphones are able to accurately recognize objects, animals or monuments. The phones then display several pieces of information about what they recognize.[22]

In some smartphone models, the photo sensor is able to recognize what it will photograph (an animal, a flower, a human being...) and it will search in the millions of photos to which it has access, a similar photo and thus make the right settings.

Companies are not left out. We all know chatbots (chat as in online discussion, and bot as in robot), small chatty robots that answer our questions according to a well-defined tree structure. They can be found on the websites of SNCF, Amtrak, Orange, Fnac, Ikea

20 Paul Guyonnet, *"La reconnaissance faciale de l'iPhone X peut servir à essayer des lunettes,"* *Huffington Post*, 08/11/2017.
21 http://theconversation.com/etude-de-cas-la-reconnaissance-faciale-integree-a-la-publicite-digitale-94382
22 Anouch Seydtaghia, *"L'intelligence artificielle est déjà omniprésente dans nos vies"*, *Le Temps*, 08/01/2018.

and other companies.

There are many examples and they affect all areas of society. A recent study by the Boston Consulting Group23 provides a classification of AI usage scenarios.

Computer Vision and Perception

- Autonomous vehicles
- Medical diagnostics by image analysis
- Inspection system (e.g. default detection

Natural Language

- Personal assistants (Google Home, Alexa)
- Chatbot (customer service, sales)
- Automated document analysis, translation

Robotics

- Production optimization
- Optimization of logistics
- Robotic Shared Services Center

Decision Support

- Personalization of offers and recommendation
- Predictive analysis (e.g. maintenance)
- Fraud prevention and detection

Examples: AI in Companies

Banks

Some banks, such as Crédit Mutuel, use Watson, IBM's Artificial Intelligence, to help their 20,000 account managers

---

23 Boston Consulting group & Malakoff Méderic, "*Intelligence Artificielle et Capital Humain*", March 2018.

reply to e-mails and consolidate their knowledge of insurance and savings offers. In concrete terms, Watson can answer customer service representatives' questions about offers, saving them the time and effort of searching internal documentary databases. Watson is also connected to the messaging of advisers to detect urgent e-mails and suggest customizable answers.24

Elevators

When you use a KONE25 elevator, it is equipped with Artificial Intelligence, in particular to manage predictive maintenance. KONE maintains more than one million elevators and escalators worldwide, enabling a billion people to move around every day. Artificial Intelligence can analyze the connected sensors in each elevator. If the AI discovers a potential problem, technicians are immediately notified. Therefore, maintenance measures are taken before the symptoms become problems. You can even watch live conversations from the elevators with Watson (IBM Artificial Intelligence)26.

Cosmetics

The American cosmetics brand Kiehl's uses Artificial Intelligence via predictive models to anticipate the usage speed of a product and suggest to the customer to reorder the product, at the right time, by e-mail, on Facebook Messenger and soon by SMS. The customer is prompted to answer with a simple "Yes" or "Remind me later," explains Laurence Faguer, FrenchWeb27 retail expert.

Electronics

At the Japanese electronics manufacturer Hitachi, warehouse workers have begun working with AI. They take their instructions from this system in order to increase their productivity. The computer analyzes how employees have approached different problems in the past. When an employee

24 « Le Crédit Mutuel accélère dans l'intelligence artificielle", Les Échos, 20/04/2017.
25 www.kone.fr
26 machineconversations.kone.com/
27 https://www.frenchweb.fr/lintelligence-artificielle-sinvite-avec-justesse-chez-kiehls/320176

uses a new approach, it is immediately analyzed and integrated for later use. This approach is based on the Kaizen method, based on continuous improvement. Rather than relying on pre-programed instructions as with classic software, Hitachi explains that this AI can break out of preconceived scenarios by adapting to live changes, based on control changes or other unforeseen events.

Medicine

Artificial Intelligence platforms make it possible to monitor patients' use of drugs outside the hospital.28 These platforms are based on visual recognition. The doctor can then know precisely the conditions (time, quantity, regularity...) under which the patient has taken or not their treatment, and the patient itself has a reassuring monitoring tool.29

Air Transport

Air France offers its customers a baggage assistant, Louis, a conversational robot that answers all the questions of its interlocutors on topics related to baggage. Its role is to answer all questions regarding baggage, from company policy before departure to baggage tracking after the flight.30

For the BCG, "AI will become one of the keys to the world to come. Indeed, we are increasingly in a digital world [...] A world of data. This data, which is at the heart of the functioning of today's Artificial Intelligence. In this world of ours, these technologies represent much more than a research program: they determine our ability to organize knowledge, give it meaning, and increase our ability to make decisions and control systems. And in particular to draw from the value of data. Artificial Intelligence is therefore one of the keys to the power of tomorrow in a digital world."31

28 aicure.com/
29 www.ouest-france.fr/sante/en-medecine-les-impacts-reels-de-l-intelligence- artificielle-5449707
30 www.usine-digitale.fr/article/air-france-lance-louis-son-premier-chatbot-bagages-le-premier-d-une-longue-lignee.n619853
31 BCG, "Intelligence Artificielle et Capital Humain - Quels défis pour les entreprises ?", March 2018.

Chapter 2

Artificial Intelligence and Employment

"It is work that humanizes the world."[32]

32 Nicolas Bouzou, *Le travail est l'avenir de l'homme*, Édition l'Observatoire, 2017

Work is Not Disappearing, it is Transforming

The idea that machines will make human work obsolete is spreading. Will we soon see the end of human work? Between apocalyptic predictions and digital naïve optimism, analyses diverge. The impact of AI on employment at the societal level is likely to be significant but remains complex to analyze.

"If it is not established that the development of Artificial Intelligence constitutes a fourth industrial revolution per se, it nevertheless appears more and more certain that it will modify the majority of professions and organizations. This development will allow the automation of a large number of tasks. We are therefore entering a period of major technological transition, which is not without raising major concerns: history teaches us that previous transitions have not been smooth and that political readjustment processes have sometimes been violent, often to the detriment of the already most fragile populations."[33]

In 2013, two Oxford researchers estimated that self-sufficiency represented a risk for 47% of jobs.[34] A more recent study by the OECD[35] found that the threat is much lower. For the OECD, robotization is only a threat to 9% of jobs, those where at least 70% of their tasks can be automated.

History disproves all alarmist predictions: technological innovation has always created more jobs than it has eliminated in the end. It is undeniable that innovation destroys jobs, but it is a process of destruction-substitution-creation. Automation did not wait until the 21st century to impact our ways of working without completely eliminating the workforce in a sector of activity. As a reminder, it is possible to fly an aircraft without a pilot since 1945. However, there are about 250,000 aircraft pilots in operation today, and Boeing expects that half a million additional pilots will be hired worldwide in the next 20 years, explains Dennis Pennel.[36]

---

33 www.aiforhumanity.fr/pdfs/9782111457089_Rapport_Villani_accessible.pdf
34 Carl Benedikt Frey and Michael A. Osborne, September 2013.
www.oxfordmartin.ox.ac.uk/downloads/academic/the_Future_of_Employment.pdf
35 M. Arntz, T. Gregory, U. Zierahn, "The risk of Automation for Jobs in OECD Countries", OCDE, May 2016.
36 Mag RH, "Les RH et l'IA : les Robots de l'aube", 08/12/2017.

Destruction-Substitution-Creation Cycle

A recent study by the consulting firm McKinsey[37] estimates that 45% of tasks could be automated with current technologies, but only 5% of jobs would be at risk of being completely replaced. Automation does not eliminate jobs so much as it substitutes itself for people on certain tasks, redesigning production processes and requiring new skills to be mastered. This learning of new processes and know-how requires investments in capital, training and time.

On the other hand, we have a tendency - quite naturally – to digitize the present, but we are absolutely unable to imagine the workplace of tomorrow and the day after tomorrow. Who could have imagined ten years ago the arrival of professions such as webmaster, data scientist, data protection manager, YouTuber, community manager, corporate happiness manager? Most of the jobs our children will be doing do not yet exist...

Technology clearly creates jobs when it allows the creation of completely new industries. This is perfectly demonstrated in Robert Atkinson's[38] study of the labor market between 1850 and 2015. The trade examples chosen in this study may seem outdated (conductor and automotive engineers), but it has the merit of being very informative and, above all, of offering sufficient perspective over more than a century to validate the mechanism of communicating vessels in the labor market.

This study reveals a dramatic increase in employment in the railway industry in the 1850s in the United States.

Between 1850 and 1860, the number of locomotive engineers, drivers and conductors increased by almost 600% and continues to increase for the rest of the century. But this growth fell before the 1920s, partly because rail transport became more productive (and therefore needed fewer operators).

At the same time, the automotive industry has begun to gain market share on rail transport.

Since 1920, railway occupations have declined steadily every decade.

---

37 www.mckinsey.com/business-functions/digital-mckinsey/our-insights/where-machinescould-replace-humans-and-where-they-cant-yet - July 2016.
38 Robert Atkinson, "False Alarmism: Technological Disruption and the US Labor Market, 1850-2015", 2017

However, since the 2000s, the number of mobile car workers has also declined, perhaps partly because the mechanical quality of cars has improved significantly, and they require fewer repairs.

A McKinsey study comes to the same conclusion, with, for example, the impact of the arrival of the personal computer (PC) on the American labor market.

As we can see, there is a job rotation rate, which Robert Atkinson also measured over a decade. It shows that this turnover rate has been the lowest in U.S. history for several decades, reaching its peak in 1960. This low level is quite surprising considering the turmoil of the 2000s: the Internet bubble, the great recession, the subprime crisis and the continuing challenge of trade with China. Does the massive arrival of AI herald a renewal of this job rotation?

For Europe, the OECD[39] reaches the same conclusion. Over the 1999-2010 period, in 27 European countries, the impact of job rotation due to technological change was 9.6 million substituted jobs, offset by 21.1 million new jobs, for a net positive effect of 11.6 million jobs

A recent study by KPMG International[40] confirms this optimistic view. 62% of CEOs surveyed in this study believe that AI will create more jobs than it will eliminate.

The scale of these changes could be significant and unprecedented since the transition of the non-agricultural labor force in the early 1900s in the United States and Europe, and more recently in China. This is potentially 375 million workers that could have to change occupational groups and learn new skills. For so-called advanced economies, the number of workers expected to acquire these new skills and change jobs is much higher than in the rest of the world: up to one third of the labor force in 2030 in the United States and Germany and almost half in Japan.[41] The challenge will be particularly important for mid-career workers. Indeed, we can imagine that young workers will be able to adapt more easily to a

39 Gregory, Salomons et Zierahn, "Racing with or Against the Machine? Evidence from Europe", July 2016
40 "2018 Gobal CEO Outlook," KPMG International.
41 www.mckinsey.com/global-themes/future-of-organizations-and-work/what-the-future-ofwork-will-mean-for-jobs-skills-and-wages#part%201

digitalized world since birth, while employees at the end of their careers will gradually leave the workplace to enjoy their retirement.

In their book, *The Second Machine Age* [42], Erik Brynjolfsson and Andrew McAfee explain, quite conventionally, that technological progress is evolving exponentially. But they also hold that the second age of the machine (the first was that of the Industrial Revolution) does the same for intellectual capacity... What the steam engine did for muscle power, Artificial Intelligence allows us to do it with our cognitive functions; allowing us to overcome our limitations and discover new territories.

What about employment in all this? Resolutely optimistic, McAfee and Brynjolfsson believe that "humans are still more skilled than most of the most advanced robots, and that this will continue to be the case for a long time to come." They are campaigning for a man-machine cooperation. It would therefore not be necessary to be alarmed by the end of work, but to do everything possible to prepare for its future.

"In essence, machines are doing what they do best: performing repetitive tasks, analyzing huge data sets, and handling routine cases. And humans are doing what they do best: resolving ambiguous information, exercising judgment in difficult cases, and dealing with dissatisfied customers. "[43]

In truth, machines do not take control of the world, and do not replace humans in the workplace. At a time of profound transformations in our business processes, AI systems do not replace us, but they amplify our skills and collaborate with us to achieve productivity gains that were not previously possible.

42 Erik Brynjolfsson et Andrew McAfee, *Le Deuxième âge de la machine, Travail et prospérité à l'heure de la révolution technologique*, Éditions Odile Jacob, 2015.
43 Paul Daugherty et H. James Wilson, Human + Machine, Reimagining Work in the Age of AI, HBR Review Press, 2018.

Chapter 3

The HRD, Bringing Meaning to Work

"It is not necessarily natural for a professional to work with a cognitive system. [...] Given the importance of this impact, it is essential to support employees and teach them how to use this type of system."

Human Resources Directors (HRDs) are on the front line to facilitate the implementation of AI by anticipating its human impacts. HR faces five major challenges:

- **Understanding the specificities of the transformations due to AI** for each company, according to their size and maturity in digital data, and taking into account the extent of anticipated disruptions. It is essential to make it a subject of discussion within management teams, but also of collective debates and social dialogue within the company.

- Foreseeing, as the multiplicity of impacts will raise a question of overall coherence in terms of sites, companies, branches, territories and at the national level; war for talents is being prepared on certain profiles, desertion of certain skills in regions, extent of restructuring on profiles with low or average quality, large-scale requalification of employees... Companies that will have readied themselves will be those that will benefit from the AI transformation.

- **Creating a culture of trust** with employees, by setting up the conditions for an AI ethic. Strengthening the ethics function within companies, which should go well beyond regulatory issues but focus on the values that the companies want to promote.

- More fundamentally, it will be a question of **giving meaning to** the deployment of AI: adapting the company's culture, supporting changes in professional identities, but also reinventing employee expression, in particular - but not unanimously - through social dialogue, to support flatter, more transparent, less hierarchical and more cooperative forms of organization.

- Finally, the **HR function itself will be profoundly disrupted** by the opportunities offered by AI. The augmented HRD will have to consider the generalization of the human-machine pair and will have to integrate the contribution of machines to effectively fulfill its new role.[44]

This level of challenge makes AI a subject of General Management, of which HRDs will be the strong arm. The latter are

---

44 BCG, *"Intelligence Artificielle et Capital Humain,"* March 2018.

becoming aware of the vast project that is opening up for their teams: shedding light on the respective fields of human tasks and AI tasks, setting up safeguards to supervise human-machine collaboration, strengthening the relational aspects of the affected jobs, setting up indicators that will make it possible to finely understand the impacts of the generalization of AI in the workplace...

Meeting these challenges requires a rapid launch of a large number of actions in various fields. In this second part, we draw up a first list, to be adapted by organization and according to company size.

Strengthening the Ethics Function Within Companies

"The 21st-century business will be the one that takes full advantage of the potential of Artificial Intelligence, and at the same time chooses to place human value at the heart of its model."[45]

In its recent report, the CNIL explains that ethical reflection on AI systems and algorithms only makes sense if it also takes into account their inclusion in social, human and professional contexts.[46]

There is a widespread belief that algorithms are objective because they use a large amount of data. Nothing could be further from the truth. AI is not detached from Human Intelligence. Algorithms are written and maintained by humans an automatic learning algorithm adjust their actions based on human behavior. The algorithms of Artificial Intelligence systems work without question, depending on their programming and the training they have received. Unfortunately, this can lead to discriminatory situations. As a result, algorithms may very well reinforce human prejudices. Without even being aware of it, we could teach and transmit our prejudices to AIs.

Another point of attention related to algorithms is the creation of the Filter Bubble. The filter bubble refers both to the information that reaches the Internet user through different filters, and the state

45 Pascal Demurger, Managing Director of the MAIF Group.
46 CNIL Report, *"Comment permettre à l'homme de garder la main,"* December 2017.

of *intellectual isolation* and cultural isolation in which they find themselves when the information they seek on the Internet or another computer system results from a personalization implemented without their knowledge. As in an *echo chamber*, this phenomenon tends to be self-sustaining by reproducing the user's opinions, beliefs and perspectives in a vicious circle.[47]

It is essential to think of the ethics at the same time as the technological development. No company deploying AI will be able to avoid this question.

It is obvious that operational staff will not be able to answer these ethical questions alone. A new essential function will therefore appear in executive committees: that of Chief Ethics Officers or Chief Value Officers or, in French, le *Déontologue*.

It is also a strong recommendation of the CNIL which suggests six operational variations to public authorities:

- Training all the links in the *algorithmic chain* (designers, professionals, citizens) in ethics.
- Making algorithmic systems understandable by strengthening existing rights and organizing mediation with users.
- Working on the design of algorithmic systems for human freedom.
- Providing a national platform for auditing algorithms.
- Encouraging research on ethical AI and launching a major national participatory cause around a research project of general interest.
- Strengthening the ethical function within companies. In her excellent book *Des Robots et des Hommes*[48], Laurence Devillers offers four pillars in the reflection on ethics:
- **Educate researchers** and designers but also reporters, politicians and as many people as possible about the ethics of robots.
- **Explain the rules** of good conduct to be coded onto robots and design it to be able to learn them continuously.
- **Implement tools** to verify that the robot complies with the rules.

47 wikipedia.org/wiki/Filter_bubble
48 Laurence Devillers, *Des Robots et des Hommes*, Plon, 2017.

- **Have a set of legal regulations** in case of non-compliance with the rules.

The role of the deontologist, and/or their committee, will therefore be to identify possible irregularities or harmful effects prior to the deployment of algorithms.

In addition, it will have to ensure a continuous monitoring role to identify emerging problems, imperceptible at the outset, *weak signals*, providing an alternative to the vision of operational staff.

Several implementation methods could be considered, under the impetus of the Human Resources Departments:

- The deployment of ethics committees within companies utilizing algorithms with significant impacts.
- The attribution of the deontological aspect to the CSR[49] function.
- The establishment of ethical networks organized by sectors or professional branches to ensure the dissemination of good practices and the early identification of emerging problems. They will also be able to carry out an ethical watch, with the creation, in the long term, of sectoral ethical guidelines (ethical charters, codes of conduct, deontological charters, etc.) and revise pre-existing professional codes of ethics to consider the introduction of AI.
- The creation of a chapter dedicated to the issues raised by algorithms in deontological charters of companies (by clarifying, for example, the limits not to be crossed when designing system parameters, quality and accessibility obligations for the data sets used to train algorithms, etc.).
- The implementation of governance on ethical issues in the company, by opening up the ethical debate to all stakeholders.

"Faced with the upcoming upheavals brought about by AI and by digital training in general, it is necessary to set up an ethical charter within HR," says Jérémy Lamri, co-founder of Lab RH, speaking at the *L'Intelligence Artificielle comme levier de performance de la fonction RH* conference.[50]

Thus, Lab RH51 proposes an Ethical & Digital HR Charter in order to establish a framework of best practices for the use of digital

49 Corporate Social Responsibility.
50 jobsferic.fr/Salon-Solutions-RH-2018-intelligence-artificielle-RGPD-start-up-innovantes.html
51 Lab RH, a 1901 association, promotes HR innovation in all its forms, thanks to its 420 members, https://www.lab-rh.com/

solutions in the field of Human Resources, so that the rights, freedoms and sensitivities of everyone are respected.

During its round table on Artificial Intelligence and Human Resources on June 14, 2017, the CFE-CGC conducted a survey among its activists (1,263 respondents). While many were concerned about the loss of human control (63%), 92% made it a priority to establish an ethical charter around the use of algorithms in recruitment and HR management.

This charter was drafted under the impetus of the CFE-CGC, then the Lab HR, in collaboration with the CNIL, the Ministry of Labor, Employment, Vocational Training and Social Dialogue, and the Secretariat of Digital Data. It is available for viewing online.[52]

For its part, CERNA (*Commission de réflexion sur l'Éthique de la Recherche en science et technologie du Numérique d'Allistene*[53]) also produced a report on the ethics of robotics researchers in 2017. CERNA's vocation is to speak out on the ethics of research in digital science and technology and aims to encourage and assist researchers to be vigilant in their ethical conduct rather than to issue normative prescriptions that would quickly become obsolete.[54]

SWP is Becoming more Important

"We are gradually moving from a world of programming to a world of learning."[55]

Strategic Workforce Planning (SWP) is the anticipation and planning of the company's strategy, and the assessment of the skills required to carry out the business plan. In a context of constant evolution, the company must continuously adapt its Human Capital.

---

52 parlement-et-citoyens.fr/projects/petition-legislative/collect/deposit-your-petition/proposals/charte-ethique-amp-numeric-rh
53 Allistene: Alliance des Sciences et technologies du numérique.
54 cerna-ethics-allistene.org/digitalAssets/53/53991_cerna___thique_apprentissage.pdf
55 Jean-Philippe Desbiolles, IBM, event to launch the public debate, CNIL, 23 January 2017 - CNIL Report *"Comment permettre à l'homme de garder la main."*

Evolution of Skills

The evolution of skills and jobs in relation to AI is a new field of investigation for Human Resources Directors.

"The knowledge-based approach of '200 years ago,' would 'fail our kids,' who would never be able to compete with machines. Children should be taught 'soft skills' like independent thinking, values and team-work," says Jack Ma, founder of Alibaba, a Chinese e-commerce giant.[56]

A study by the World Economic Forum in Davos shows a change in the order of key competences in a very short period of time: critical thinking and creativity take over the top positions. There is also the integration of emotional intelligence and cognitive flexibility. With the arrival of AI, we are witnessing a disruption in the hierarchy of competencies: transversal, social and situational competencies become key.

On closer examination, it is a question of massively developing the complementary human skills of Artistic Intelligence, or at least the non-substitutable ones. The automation of tasks and professions can constitute a historical opportunity for the de-automatization of human work: it allows the development of uniquely human capacities (creativity, manual dexterity, abstract thinking, problem solving).

The study by the *Conseil d'Orientation pour l'Emploi* (COE)[57] confirms these analyses: it shows that social skills (teamwork, social intelligence) and situational skills (autonomy, learning to learn) are on average increasingly in demand in a digital work environment.

It is interesting to note that these skills do not require expertise in machine learning or programming. Rather, it is about being thoughtful humans who want to adapt to the fundamental skills of their profession.

For the authors Paul R. Daugherty and H. James Wilson in *Human + Machine*[58], human-machine collaboration requires the

---

56 www.weforum.org/agenda/2018/01/top-quotes-from-davos-on-the-future-of-education/
57 www.coe.gouv.fr/Synthese_Report_Automatisation_numerisation_et_emploi_tome_2a993.pdf
58 Paul R. Daugherty, H. James Wilson, Human + Machine, Reimagining Work at the age of IA, *HBR Review press*, 2018.

development of eight fusion skills.

Each of these skills reinforces the fusion between man and machine to improve the results of a business process. What differs from previous eras is precisely the human-machine interaction: the machine learns from you and you learn from it, thus creating a virtuous circle of process improvement.

These fusion skills are as follows[59]:

1. **Rehumanizing Time**: the ability to use one's available time for socialization, creation and decision-making tasks.

2. **Responsible Normalizing**: being able to normalize, in a responsible way, the objectives and perception of human-machine interactions when they concern individuals, society, and business.

3. **Judgment Integration**: the ability to decide on a course of action when the machine is uncertain about the task to be performed.

4. **Intelligent Interrogation**: knowing what question to ask the AI, with different levels of abstraction, to get the answers you need.

5. **Bot-Based Empowerment**: being able to work with intelligent agents to extend your capabilities, accelerate business processes and develop your professional career.

6. **Holistic Melding**: the ability to develop robust cognitive models to maximize the results of intellectual agents. This is the case, for example, when you experience the feeling of using a tool as easily as if it were an extension of your body or mind.

7. **Reciprocal Apprenticing**: (i) The user performs tasks alongside Artificial Intelligence so that both can learn; (ii) Employee training makes it easier to work with AI.

8. **Imagination**: the ability to create new processes and models from scratch, rather than simply automating old processes.

This last skill reflects the very essence of human-machine collaboration. It would be totally useless to breathe AI into our old ways of organizing work. We must use the opportunity offered by AI to reinvent everything.

---

59 List adapted from the book Human + Machine.

Participatory Approach

Users will need to be involved at all hierarchical and cross-functional levels to work on the SWP[60]. The place given to co-construction on this subject will determine the future adoption of AI projects in the company.

This participatory approach has two advantages:

- it is the employees who are best able to evaluate the different dimensions of their activities at work, to integrate their experience and thus propose improvements to the existing system;

it makes it possible to become an actor and to move from a sudden step to a projective step, guaranteeing a better adoption of the future work situation.

The HRD can therefore encourage everyone's contribution and organize discussions on transformation. Of course, mandatory negotiations are also part of its organized discussions.

Author Stéphane Mallard, in his book *Disruption*, explains that to meet this need for empathy, companies must be prepared and "will have to recruit and train for emotional excellence. They will have to work with psychologists, philosophers, artists and other soft skills professionals to learn to put themselves in the shoes of their clients and create this exceptional relationship."[61]

Training

Faced with the evolution of required skills, the implementation of appropriate training plans is an urgent matter. Especially since, according to a recent Accenture study, only 3% of executives say they intend to increase their training investments over the next three years.[62]

However, this formidable project raises a number of preliminary questions:

- How to define these transversal competences?

60 Strategic Workforce Planning
61 Stéphane Mallard, *Disruption*, Dunod, 2018.
62 Accenture, "Future Workforce Worker and C-Suite Surveys," 2017.

- How to recognize them (on the internal market but also on the external labor market in a logic of employability)?
- What certifications?
- How to identify them: which repository to use?
- How can they be measured objectively?
- How to recognize the different levels of progress?
- How can they be used to guide recruitment and mobility?
- How can they be adopted by the various stakeholders: employees, managers, employee representative bodies, training organizations, etc.?

For employees, there is little choice: it is a matter of engaging in life-long learning. *Learning to learn* will become essential. Indeed, the technological flow profoundly modifies the content of jobs, the use of AI requires it (questioning, doubt, experimentation, etc.) and the technologies themselves are constantly evolving, very quickly in our *VUCA*[63] world. It refers to the current environment (volatile, uncertain, complex and ambiguous), and highlights the difficulty of making decisions in a complex and uncertain environment. Faced with this environment, the future undoubtedly belongs to those who can learn and unlearn.

Reviewing the Content of Training from the Perspective of Cognitive Functions

Unfortunately, the time dedicated to training to develop transversal skills and employability is often restrained in our companies, with priority often being given to technical training.

Continuous training therefore faces a challenge: the transition to a model for the development of transversal skills and employability. This is a true pivot of the current model.

In this context, HRDs will have four equations to solve:

- How to free up time on business training plans already occupied by regulatory obligations to develop employees' transversal skills?
- How to develop the employability of employees without

---

63 Volatility, Uncertainty, Complexity, Ambiguity.

degrading the quality of service and customer commitment?

- With what content and in what format should the pre-eminence of transversal competences be brought to life?
- What will be the impact of AI-based tools on the training exercise itself?

Players are Mobilizing to Create a Learning Society

The *France Apprenante* coalition[64] brings together actors in the fields of education, learning, innovation, digital data and training (the Openclassrooms platform, the Numa accelerator, 42 schools and Simplon, the Schoolab innovation studio and the Lab RH initiative) who wish to support the transformation of territories and companies by making new ways of learning accessible to all. It was launched on 16 May 2018 to meet the challenges of training in the coming years.

■ The objective of France Apprenante

France Apprenante is deploying solutions on a large scale to build a learning society by bringing together formidable innovation capacities that exist in our country to make them accessible to all.

Within a decade, Artificial Intelligence and robotization will have eliminated most professional activities with little added value. The talents who invent the society of tomorrow will be those who dare to be entrepreneurial, who know how to work in a team and who master digital technology.

It is no longer a question of learning by deploying heavy and lengthy training programs, but rather of learning to learn, that is, to ensure that everyone becomes an actor in their own development through efficient methods to train in quality and quantity.

"According to the OECD, we will move from a training model that is essentially based on knowledge acquisition to one that integrates the development of tomorrow's skills. Like critical thinking, creativity, communication and collaboration," says Boris Sirbey, spokesperson for Lab RH.[65]

---

64 Website: franceapprenante.com
65 business.lesechos.fr/entrepreneurs/idees-de-business/0301684784534-france-apprenanteune-coalition-pour-transformer-la-formation-en-profondeur-320973.php

Rethinking Professional Careers

"Professional careers will have to be rethought in their entirety." The training of employees will have to be thoroughly reviewed so that they develop "behavioral and relational skills, even [...] cognitive skills."66

The articulation of professional careers will therefore be separated from the traditional job description. These paths will be more diffuse, hybrid, showing a certain porosity, and more oriented towards skills, and, in particular, cognitive skills. Thus, it would become possible to recruit by measuring only these cognitive skills and by freeing oneself from trade skills. This would greatly reduce the labor market. Indeed, cognitive functions could serve as a foundation to identify talent pools in the market or internally.

The standards of initial training and diplomas considered relevant by the branches or sectors will have to be reviewed quickly to respond to a more transversal approach.

In addition, the evaluation of performance in the position held, which is a key criterion in professional careers, would be made difficult by the predominance of transversal skills over technical skills, in the absence of appropriate benchmarks and an evaluation matrix.

Good news! It will probably be easier than today to find a job outside your primary sector of activity, or inversely, to enter it during your professional career. The mixing of profiles should be more important, externally and internally.

This perspective of evolution raises questions especially for the median generation of employees (35-50 years old). Indeed, younger ones have had less time to acquire strong "occupational" skills and are on average open to the idea of less linear paths.

Older ones, on the other side, will probably have the opportunity to finish their careers before major AI impacts are at work.67

---

66 www.observatoire-metiers-banque.fr/f/etudes/sf/plus/s/IA_emploi_
competences_banque?utm_content=buffera4bd3&utm_medium=social&utm_source=twitter.c
om&utm_ campaign=buffer
67 http://www.gref-bretagne.com/Actualites/Revue-de-presse/Intelligence-artificielle.-
Quels-impacts-sur-les-metiers-et-les-competences-du-secteur-bancaire

Towards the Disappearance of Job Descriptions?

According to an Accenture survey68, 46% of executives surveyed believe that job descriptions are obsolete.

Typically, traditional job descriptions cover a list of tasks, skills, performance indicators, and of salary packages. They date from the first industrial era69... and participate in the structuring of the company according to a vertical hierarchy, based mainly on the delegation of tasks. The result is the installation of a certain routine, unused skills and frightened employees who are afraid to leave their perimeter of intervention.70

Today, and even more so with AI, work is organized into projects. This approach to work, which is less hierarchical and less compartmentalized in terms of skills, calls into question the very idea of defining the limits of a position. This approach involves focusing on the employee's adaptability and professional and human qualities, before their ability to perform tasks. Within a project, the distribution of tasks will be done according to the capacities of each person, in a way similar to volunteering.

"In the future, candidates may be hired for several roles at a time. Talent will be non-linear - less related to skills and more related to thinking. A human resources department will no longer compose teams according to checklists but on a deeper matrix of interests, intellectual backgrounds, past experiences and cultural points of view."71

68 Accenture, " Reworking the revolution future workforce."
69 hbr.org/2017/04/thinking-through-how-automation-will-affect-your-workforce
70 www.forbes.fr/management/le-travail-en-mode-projet-signe-t-il-la-fin-des-fiches-de-workstations/?cn-reloaded=1
71 Remy Demichelis, "Comment les dirigeants perçoivent l'intelligence artificielle," Les Échos, 10/09/2018.

The New AI Professions

To use the old Latin saying, errare humanum est: error is human; the machine is perfect, only man makes mistakes. But only humans can correct their mistakes... And only humans know how to detect the inadequacies of machines and evaluate the relevance or inadequacy of their use.[72]

As we have seen previously, the progress of AI will impact and kill a number of professions, but at the same time others will appear to program, educate and manage it. It is obvious that Artificial Intelligence will have to be integrated into our daily lives and work. A study by Dell and the Institute for the Future, an American think tank, reports that 85% of jobs in 2030 do not yet exist.[73]Today, the majority of AI jobs are in engineering, but in the near future, management, educators and psychologists will be considered. It is necessary to rethink the organization of work and the distribution of tasks.

According to a study by the BCG and Malakoff Médéric[74], AI-related jobs can be classified into three categories:

- Jobs directly related to AI in companies, data science, process analysts, AI production jobs; for example: designers, integrators...
- Jobs allowed by AI, related to new modes of functioning ("generalists, specialists in human relations, empathy") or related technologies ("augmented reality designer...").
- Jobs related to new products and services that AI provides.

In Human + Machine, the authors propose an alternative approach to new corporate roles in the deployment of AI[75]:

- The role of Trainer[76]: their mission will be to train Artificial Intelligence on their workstation. A chatbot, for example, must be trained to understand the subtleties of human communication.
- The role of Explainer: their mission will be to make the link between the technological teams and the business. They will bring

72 Jean-Gabriel Ganascia, *Intelligence Artificielle, vers une domination programmée ?*, Edition Le Cavalier Bleu, 2017.
73 www.delltechnologies.com/content/dam/delltechnologies/assets/perspectives/2030/pdf/SR1940_IftfforDelltechnologies_Human-Machine_070517_readerhigh-res.pdf
74 media-publications.bcg.com/Intelligence-artificielle-et-capital-humain.pdf
75 sloanreview.mit.edu/article/will-ai-create-as-many-jobs-as-it-eliminates/
76 www.nytimes.com/2017/04/28/technology/meet-the-people-who-train-the-robots-to-do-their-own-jobs.html

more clarity, thus reducing the anxiety associated with the impression of a "Black Box" that AI can sometimes generate.

- The role of Sustainer: their mission will be to ensure that the AI operates as it should and address potential risks and problems with appropriate urgency.

Setting Up Work Transformation Labs

In his report "Giving meaning to Artificial Intelligence," Cédric Villani proposes the creation of a public lab for the transformation of work.

"It is [...] necessary to create a space where forward-looking capacities, macroeconomic forecasts and analysis of changes in uses can be linked with concrete and articulated experimentation capacities with actions aimed at certain categories of workers. A permanent structure could therefore be set up, that would have a *homing device* role within public employment and vocational training policies. A close link should be maintained with branch observers."

In the same way that Fab Labs (*Fabrication Laboratories*) are places open to the public, where all kinds of computer tools are made available for the design and production of objects, Work Transformation Labs could help build the jobs of tomorrow.

It seems interesting to apply this idea in the company. Why not imagine smaller-scale work transformation labs, where everyone can come and exchange, debate and build tomorrow's jobs within the company? This is somewhat the approach adopted by Société Générale, which relies on a self-assessment platform available to its employees called Monjob2020, which allows you to assess your skills and project yourself into your *job of the future*. "We want to give visibility to our employees because the transformation we are undergoing is anxiety-provoking," says Laurent Goutard, head of Société Générale retail banking.[77]

---

77 Les Échos, "Formation : les banques face au défi des métiers de demain," 06/07/2018.

Chapter 4

Human-Machine Collaboration

"Our teams welcome these new types of
employees with great kindness."[78]

---

78 Bruno Kauffman, Director of Industrial Soltion at Hager:
www.man-and-machine.staubli.com/en/man-and-machine/

The Cobot, Your New Colleague

Human-machine relationship is now entering a new era that goes far beyond strict robotization. Experts estimate that, by 2030, new relationships between man and machine will gradually emerge.

Both are described as complementary *beings*. The balance of power therefore tends to be reversed towards more collaboration and not dependence. These *partnerships* will thus have "a significant impact on both individuals and organizations."[79] We will see the emergence of integrated man-machine teams that will operate through multimodal, enhanced and transparent interfaces. For some consulting firms, such as Gartner for example, this man-machine partnership relationship will happen very quickly: some projections show that 1 in 5 workers will have Artificial Intelligence as a colleague in 2022!

Of course, the human-machine relationship is far from new. But with AI, we are entering a new phase in this relationship, in which this distribution is no longer obvious: in some cases, the machine decides what actions and tasks to perform. This changes the content and organization of work. The challenge for HR is therefore to invent a harmonious and intelligent cohabitation/collaboration between humans and machines. The risk of AI is to reinforce individualization, the loss of know-how, the development of micro-control, the disengagement of people, the feeling of loneliness, the devaluation of work, even a form of proletarianization of jobs... It is necessary to protect oneself from the risks of AI and therefore to accompany change, to ensure that they operate as a duo and not in duel.

We are talking about cobotics (a neologism resulting from the contraction of the words *robotics* and *collaboration*) or collaborative robotics. Collaboration is based on an optimal combination of everyone's strengths:

- Robots perform repetitive tasks with power, durability and precision.
- Humans use their know-how, their perception of things, their sensitivity, their experience, to take on tasks that are less mechanical, less precise, where their thinking and action bring

---

79 Dell and Vanson Bourn Study, February 2018.

added value.

Robots leave protective cages and are now able to take an object and give it to a human. They also have learning characteristics.

The interaction with the robot will be done by voice but also by contact, to correct its movement or to train it and show it what is expected of it. AI will allow them to grasp what they need to do.

In 2017, the DHL Group, which specializes in transport and logistics, integrated collaborative robots into its production process. On a co-packing application designed for DHL, the robots work directly on the production line. Robots in DHL warehouses can navigate through a complex structure and perform multiple tasks. They work safely alongside the operators. They are in charge of repetitive or even dangerous tasks, freeing up the operator's time so that they can work on tasks with higher added value. With the help of these robots, operator productivity has increased by 25%.[80]

Develop a New Recruitment Strategy

"Recruit for personality and train for skills."[81]

As we have just seen in the previous chapter, transversal competencies will play an important role in the development and collaboration with AI. In the context of recruitment, knowing how to identify and evaluate these skills then becomes strategic. As a result, it will be easier to recruit outside one's background branch, technical skills or even sectoral experience taking a back seat.

Addressing market shortages

Where and how do we find talent in the field of AI?

In this field and particularly in the deep learning sector, talent is scarce, and salaries are high!

This inflation is due to the limited number of talented people and the fierce competition between players in the automotive industry and digital giants.

The study conducted by the Tencent Research Institute (a Chinese

---

80 www.humarobotics.com/robots-collaboratifs-sawyer-dhl/
81 Peter Schutz, former CEO of Porsche.

technology giant)[82] indicates that the number of "researchers and practitioners of Artificial Intelligence" is estimated to be in the range of 200,000 to 300,000 people, while labor market demand is estimated to be in the millions. And according to an independent Canadian laboratory, Element AI, only 10,000 people in the world have the skills to do high-level research in the field of AI. To compensate for this lack of expert profiles, some firms rely on training, but acquiring advanced expertise requires a very high mathematical level and strong intuition.

Two ways to access AI talent[83]

- **Indirect Way**: AI researchers from the best universities are already being courted by web giants and GAFAM[84], the battle is almost lost in advance. The solution is therefore to benefit from their research work through the cloud platforms and corresponding machine learning APIs[85], which Google, AWS, Microsoft, IBM, etc., make available to the public. It remains to adapt this work to the specific needs of your organization.

Direct Way: if you want to hire your own AI researchers, there are five principles to keep in mind:

- Hunting in *virgin territories*: get off the beaten path and away from the best universities (those for which the competition is fierce...) Study the AI talent market by referring to conferences, published articles, social networks...

- Promoting diversity: work towards an egalitarian construction of the future by forming a team made up of as many women as men. This diversity will become an important factor in attracting additional talent.

- Championing flexibility: offering flexible career plans is a good way to stand out and can make a difference in attracting AI talent. Indeed, many researchers are attracted by entrepreneurial careers (the teacher in the unique position is no longer an aspiration of this population). Intrapreneurship[86] is therefore a way to attract

82 2017 Global AI Talent White Paper
83 www.fabernovel.com/insights/tech/chercheurs-dor-qui-sont-les-batisseurs-de-lia
84 Google, Apple, facebook, Amazon and Microsoft.
85 Application Programming Interface
86 Intrapreneurship: the implementation of an innovation by an employee, a group of employees or any individual working under the control of the company.

them: to allow them to keep part-time positions, or to partner with a university lab.

- Forgetting skills and recruiting personalities and learning capabilities: simply put, recruit *Potentials*, candidates with the ability to adapt and develop in an increasingly complex environment. Five qualities are reliable indicators for detecting these Potentials: motivation, curiosity, insight, commitment and determination. The talents of today will not be those of tomorrow, and the skills of today will certainly not be those we need tomorrow. The question is not whether your talent has the required skills, but whether it is able to acquire new ones. HRDs must plunge into this new era of recruitment. As Peter Schutz, former Porsche CEO, explains, it is now a question of "recruiting for personality and training for skills."

Building a holistic team: do not focus all your efforts on recruiting the Data scientist or deep learning expert, but be committed to creating a whole, a holistic team that will be mutually enriched.

The manager will therefore have to focus on the *judgment* aspect of their work. Indeed, many decisions require insight and critical thinking that goes beyond the interpretation of data, as AI can do. It is therefore key that managers complement AI with their organizational and cultural historical knowledge of the company and can demonstrate empathy and ethical reflection. This is the essence of human judgment: the application of experience and expertise to corporate decisions. Managers are the vectors of the company's culture and values on a daily basis. They will therefore have to develop skills related to creative thinking, and experimentation, in Test and Learn mode.

Team Leadership Responsibilities

The manager should be led to lead - increasingly remotely - increasingly autonomous profiles. "This new autonomy implies a rather drastic evolution of managerial practices, which is not without its difficulties," says Manuel Zacklad.[87] In addition, the teams will be mixed human-machine teams. It will then be necessary to treat intelligent machines as *colleagues*, which will avoid falling into the

---

87 Manuel Zacklad, *Intelligence Artificielle : représentations et impacts sociétaux*, CNAM, 2017.

Human versus Machine divide. The AI will then be an assistant and advisor who is always available, and can be approached in a conversational way, in a collegial way. For managers, the first challenge is to reassure people who will have AI as a colleague.

The manager of the future will have to mobilize several intelligences: individual, collective, artificial, and make sure that the intelligence of the group in the broad sense (individual + collective + AI) is greater than the sum of its parts.

If we understand how to move from an individual intelligence to a collective intelligence, the integration of AI into this collective scheme is more rational.

The first dimension of collective intelligence is cognitive. It allows the team to understand the meaning of collective action. This dimension covers: understanding, reflection and decision-making. AI will therefore be able to collaborate with this collective intelligence, which it will enrich with its predictive and even prescriptive data models.

The second dimension of collective intelligence is relational. It is a way of building relationships. This involves collaboration, autonomy (at the level of the team and individuals in the team), conflict management, development of trust and understanding. On these relational aspects, the manager will probably have to work with their team to allay fears and facilitate human-machine collaboration.

The third dimension of collective intelligence is systemic. The individual is at the center of a system and constructs their actions (contributions) by analyzing the actions of others (representations) and linking them with the system (subordinations). Crozier and Friedberg consider that it is necessary to focus, not on the function of actors or subsystems within an organization, but on the individual strategies of the actors.[88] It is rather difficult today to predict how the individual will behave in the face of AI and how the *collective system* will react. What is certain is that AI will not fit into the acting games that Crozier and Frieberg have so well described.

As we have seen above, creative skills will be key for the managers of tomorrow. It may be even more important for them to be able to stimulate the creativity of their team, to do ideation, by bringing

88 Crozier, M., Friedberg, E., *L'Acteur et le système*, Éditions du Seuil, 1977, 1981.

together ideas from different backgrounds, into integrated and pragmatic solutions. They will have to integrate *Design Thinking*[89] into their teams' daily work methods, develop entrepreneurial spirit and push them out of the box.

Their HR hat, allowing them to assess and detect the training needs of their colleagues, will have to be reinvented because, on the one hand, careers will diversify and, on the other hand, human resources departments are also developing AI tools relating - among other things - to training and mobility.

Regarding decision-making, the role of the manager will also evolve. Indeed, it will be less a question of solving problems than of finding them or at least asking the right questions to AI. The name *AI* is misleading. If the question is bad or biased, the answer will be too... The human has therefore all this room to problematize, possibly out of context.

The question of performance management also arises. The first step will be to understand how the work of employees will be impacted and what to do with all this saved time. What will be the new activities? The new occupations? If HR has an important role to play (job and skills management planning), the manager must act as a scout and start thinking about their questions beforehand, if possible, with their team.

Administrative activities will also be strongly impacted. A recent Accenture study shows that managers spend more than 50% of their time managing administrative tasks. The fact is that Artificial Intelligence will soon be able to do administrative tasks better, faster and at a lower cost. Good practice is therefore to switch over these administrative tasks to the machine: classification; organization; content curation; planification; project management; data analysis and reporting; legal, regulatory or technological monitoring.

Finally, the development of social skills and the capacity for networking will be a key to success for managers enhanced by AI: social skills, professional network management, coaching and collaboration, will help them to progress in a world where AI will manage the administrative and analytical tasks that are currently its responsibility. It is interesting, even worrying, to note that these

---

89 Design thinking is a process used by designers to innovate from existing or future uses.

social skills are nowadays largely underestimated when managers are asked about them.

In other words, the operational manager disappears, the future is for the strategist, coach, communicator and federator manager. And increased by the AI.

Faced with this change in managerial paradigm, what can we do? Simply focus on what humans can do! For starters, managers can refer to the MELDS[90] framework (Mindset, Enterprise, Leadership, Data and Skills) proposed by two American authors.

Start exploring the world of AI now! To navigate in the world of intelligent machines, managers must experiment with them, be insightful, and apply their experience iteratively.

Implement a training plan and a recruitment strategy targeted at creative, collaborative and empathic profiles now. It is necessary to set up a team with varied profiles, which will balance AI with collective and creative rational judgements. Your teams must be able to refocus on tasks with higher added value, which require creativity, reflection or diversified expertise.

It is also important to adopt new performance indicators to measure the adoption of your teams. The next criteria for measuring success will be based on the ability to collaborate, share information, experiment, learn and make effective decisions, as well as the ability to put oneself in perspective beyond the organization.

In summary, the manager of tomorrow will have to be (even more) open to the outside world to pick up signals from their environment while being (even more) turned inward to listen to their colleagues by implementing a maxim of Steve Jobs: "We don't hire intelligent people to tell them what to do, but to tell us what to do."

Whether executives or managers, we will have to improve and elevate our practices. This is not necessarily comfortable, but so exciting![91]

In their article in the Harvard Business Review[92], Erik Brynjolfsson and Andrew McAfee summarize well the challenge managers face: "In the next ten years, Artificial Intelligence will not

---

90 Paul R. Daugherty, H. James Wilson, Human + Machine, Reimagining work at the age of IA, *HBR Review Press*, 2018.
91 *"Comment l'intelligence artificielle va tirer le management vers le haut,"* Les Échos, 17/06/2017.
92 https://hbr.org/cover-story/2017/07/the-business-of-artificial-intelligence

replace managers, but the managers who use Artificial Intelligence will replace those who do not use it."

Towards a Disappearance of Managers?

Some authors, more provocative, go a step further and announce the disappearance of the role of manager. "With the arrival of Artificial Intelligence [...], managers are promoting the concept of enhanced managers. For them, algorithms allow managers to free themselves from technical and managing constraints to focus on the human being[...]. Once again, it is the same classic reflex of denial in the face of disruption: thinking that the old will remain but that it will be improved by technology or new uses. This is a mistake. Why should we want to preserve managers at all costs when disruption requires self-organization and autonomy? In an optimal company, they will disappear."[93]

This is also the opinion of Gary Hamel, lecturer and professor at the London School of Economics, author of *La Fin du management*. He refers to "office sclerosis" as management deadlock in the digital age. According to him, current management is based on a bureaucracy that tends to place managers at each hierarchical level. The weight of this hierarchy hinders internal communication and prevents creativity. Thus, if the company of tomorrow wants to be inclusive and digital, it will also have to free itself from its hierarchical chains.[94]

The concept of *liberated enterprise* also advocates the relaxation, if not the disappearance, of hierarchical structures[95]. The traditional hierarchical system is replaced by a flat structure where employees are self-directed.

93 Stéphane Mallard, Disruption, Dunod, 2018.
94 business.lesechos.fr/directions-generales/strategie/idees/0211829287771-gary-hamel-lacategorie-des-managers-va-bientot-disparaitre-306526.php
95 Issac Getz, "Liberating leadership: How the initiative-freeing radical organizational form has been successfully adopted", *California Management Review*, 2009.

Chapter 5

Integrating AI Transformation into Social Dialogue

"Faced with the arrival of Artificial Intelligence and robotics in the industry, there is only one solution for us: train yourself, train yourself, train yourself. [...] We need a general culture and we need to be trained to know how these new technologies will be integrated."[96]

---

96 Alain Giffard, Secretary General of CFE-CGC
www.usinenouvelle.com/editorial/se-former-face-a-l-intelligence-artificielle-et-la-robotique-oui-mais-comment.n592463

It is obvious that the arrival of Artificial Intelligence is a challenge for social dialogue. It is the responsibility of HRDs, in conjunction with trade unions and staff representatives, to initiate dialogue to determine the uses of AI in companies, by addressing, in parallel, the necessary issue of employee skills upgrading and quality of work life (QWL).

Unfortunately, this subject has not yet entered the field of social negotiation. Only a few pioneers have tackled it. For them, AI is one of the subjects on which co-construction with social partners will be crucial in order to instill a real dynamic to support change. Anticipating this consultation is all the more necessary as the pace of AI deployment will be rapid. AI transformation should therefore be placed at the heart of the social dialogue and the role of social partners should be strengthened. They will be able to play an active role in detecting the impact of technologies, updating skills, preserving employment, etc.

An interesting initiative, the Digilab Social aims to accelerate, through digital technology, the renewal of social and managerial dialogue, to act differently, to make life-size experiments possible in companies, and to give ideas the opportunity to prove themselves.

This lab was created at the initiative of the Secretary General and HR Director of SNCF Réseau and the Secretary General of the Union Confédérale des Cadres de la CFDT. Its mission is to better define the contours of what the functions of manager and staff representative will be in the future in a digital company and to suggest practices to be tested. The laboratory brings together, in equal parts, some fifty managers and employee representatives from companies belonging to different sectors of activity (for example Airbus, La Poste, Renault, Thalès, SNCF, EADS, Radio France and GRDF).

CFE-CGC, for its part, participated in the drafting of an HR charter (see also the chapter on Ethics in this book), by collaboration with Lab RH.97 Their thinking is based on three pillars: technology, law and morality. This charter sets out the principles laid down by the CNIL and the European Data Management and Protection Regulations. It then identifies good practices based on the four main steps that constitute the data processing chain. The first step is to capture data and then process it as such. The third aspect is the

97 www.lab-rh.com/a-propos/

restitution of the processed data and the way it is communicated. Storage and securing complete the cycle of the processing steps.[98]

It is also interesting to note that Cédric Villani's report, *Donner un sens à l'Intelligence Artificielle* [99], proposes a modification of the content of mandatory negotiations. At present, the Labor Code provides for two types of mandatory negotiations in companies, an annual one on professional equality and quality of life at work (art. L. 2242-17 of the Labor Code) and the other job and professional career management (art. L. 2242-20). In the future, the content of these negotiations could be modified and take into account "the introduction of new technologies and the digital transformation of companies, in terms of the adaptation of skills and complementarity between human and machine."

Pending changes in the content of the mandatory negotiations with social partners, here are some of the areas that could already be addressed:

- **Reflecting on Employment Trajectories**: searching for the most appropriate employment trajectories, by employment category, with stakeholders: employees themselves, trade unions, branches, suppliers, etc.
- **Rethinking Training and Requalification**: vocational training policies must accompany the introduction of new technologies, including AI, into organizations.
- **Establishing an Ethical and Deontological Framework**: the legal and regulatory framework on which companies' ethics policies would be based.

While it is key to start engaging in discussions with social partners in companies, the scale and complexity of the challenges will make it necessary to seek solutions on a broader scale (territories or professional sectors) and in relations with public authorities. Taking into account a larger ecosystem, outside traditional actors, also appears to be a good practice in this context; it will probably be necessary to dialogue with other players such as subcontractors, suppliers, customers, public authorities, local authorities,

---

98 Raphaëlle Bertholon, national delegate for l'Economie for the CFE-GSC, MAG RH, "*Les robots de l'Aube*", March 2017.
99 "*Donner un sens à l'Intelligence Artificielle - Pour une stratégie nationale et européenne*", March 2018.

universities, etc.

Company Case: How MAIF uses Artificial Intelligence to Monitor Social Climate and QWL[100]

Since 2016, the HR Communication & Social Climate Observatory Manager of the MAIF uses Proxem solutions in her listening system for employees in the service of social climate and the quality of life at work.

Thanks to digital technology, employee voices have become tangible and valuable. Artificial Intelligence makes it possible to understand and mobilize all this wealth in order to put the concerns of co-workers back at the heart of the company's digital transformation dynamics and improve well-being at work.

All processes are anonymized. This is mass-information processing, highlighting correlations, not profiling individuals. The purpose of the analysis is to describe global trends or behaviors, to assist in decision-making, rather than to describe specific and individualized behavior.

Proxem[101] is a French startup that offers an automatic language processing solution to automatically filter, analyze, tag and classify large volumes of text data, such as user comments in social networks or e-commerce sites. All this is based on machine learning and deep learning techniques. In particular, the tool allows you to explore the data analyzed visually to identify weak patterns and signals.

100 www.proxem.com/2018/02/12/petit-dejeuner-maif-utilise-lintelligence-artificielle-monitorerclimat-social-qvt/
101 www.proxem.com/

Chapter 6

HRD:

Laboratory and Model for AI Deployment

"Any scientific, philosophical, moral, political, or technological revolution goes through three stages: the stage of ridicule, the stage of danger and finally the stage of evidence."[102]

102 Idriss Aberkane, *Libérez votre cerveau !*, Robert Laffont, 2016.

Some contributions of AI to HR

While companies are beginning to use tools based on Artificial Intelligence algorithms to improve certain business processes, the use of these technologies is still limited. The question of tools will never be central (the tool does not do the process) but it is important to understand them and to rely on their power in order to transform the Human Resources Department into the Human Relations Department, for the benefit of the company and all employees.

AI has the power to improve the HR experience: it helps to improve recruitment, productivity and talent retention more effectively than traditional HR methods. At the same time, it also makes it possible to do so more quickly than ever before.

But AI tools are not a panacea and will not replace human relationships. Chatbots can replace simple administrative requests but will not replace a presence that induces other human dimensions, made of listening and empathy. These meetings are an opportunity to develop social ties with many other dimensions.

AI will use data that will allow an individualized response in almost all areas of the HR function.

A recent HR.com survey indicates that Human Resources professionals are aware that Artificial Intelligence will be part of their work environment in the near future. But the results also show that many have difficulty understanding how AI will be used and feel a lack of technical expertise to deal with these changes.

Talent Acquisition

By using AI for recruitment, the recruiter can significantly reduce their workload. Talent acquisition software can scan resumes and evaluate candidates and quickly eliminate 75% of them from the recruitment process. This automatic matching allows the recruiter to focus on evaluating a smaller group of eligible candidates and thus improve the quality of recruitment. The recruiter is still in charge, but AI allows them to speed up the process.

The arrival of AI in the recruitment field undoubtedly opens the company to more diversity, because the algorithms introduced in recruitment solutions will free candidates from the human biases that can sometimes weigh on them. This is not a value judgment, because we are all subject to biases, often unconscious, but an observation that everyone has been able to make during their professional lives.

Deferred Video Interview

Thanks to a solution of deferred video interviews, Artificial Intelligence makes it possible to carry out a behavioral analysis of the candidate.

This analysis is then compared to that of candidates previously recruited by focusing on a few key criteria: everything related, for example, to the quality of expression (lexical richness, chosen vocabulary, language register), prosody (rhythm, tone) or the way of being (smiling, dynamic, nonchalant or casual). Everything is studied to identify the candidate's emotions and the dominant aspects of their personality. The information collected in this way constitutes a database on which the recruiter can rely to assess the adequacy between the candidate's personality, the position and the company's culture.

Freedom from Cognitive Bias

This is called confirmation bias[103], which is one of the many cognitive biases to which we are all subject and which can play tricks on recruiters and interviewed candidates alike. AI can be programed to limit these biases, ignoring, for example, the candidate's age, gender or skin color to focus only on their experience, words and attitude during the interview. Algorithms can help the recruiter to overcome their own biases and identify candidates with the greatest potential for a position more quickly.[104]

In June 2017, consumer goods giant Unilever unveiled the results of a one-year trial of a video recruitment solution, *Hire View*. Between July 2016 and June 2017, 250,000 candidates from 69 different countries were interviewed in the same types of video

---

103 Confirmation bias, also known as hypothesis confirmation bias, refers to the cognitive bias of focusing on information that confirms preconceived ideas or hypotheses.
104 Mickaël Cabrol, *"Intelligence artificielle et recrutement : l'ère de la diversité"*, La Tribune, 20/12/2017.

interviews during the pre-selection phase. In addition to the gain of considerable time (the average time spent by recruiters reviewing applications decreased by 75%), the group welcomed a "significant increase in the number of non-white candidates," as well as a diversification of the applicants' social backgrounds. Unilever has also worked with the Pymetrics platform[105]: candidates spend twenty minutes playing twelve neuroscience-based games that refine their profile and ensure that they match the type of position for which they are applying.[106]

Of course, it is not a question of abandoning the recruitment process to a computing power. But algorithms put the right candidates on the recruitment track, those who are objectively the most suitable - regardless of age, gender, training, experience - and precisely what a time-sensitive recruiter would tend to do.

The recruiter then intervenes and selects the candidates according to their experience, their intuition, their intuitu personae. And, they have time to receive each candidate retained, since they did not waste time in time-consuming pre-selection phases.

Predictive Recruitment and Detection of Weak Signals

For each candidate, it is possible to know if they are in tune with the market. Thus, solutions like Yatedo are based on Artificial Intelligence. When a client is looking for a specific profile, the company screens a population similar to the job sought (same level of experience, same diploma...), using a database of more than 800 million Internet users. Then, it calculates the average time this population spends in position. Information that Yatedo cross-checks with the weak signals detected on professional social networks: profile update, status modification... A statistical approach then leads to a prediction, formulated via a percentage scoring.[107] The same approach can also be taken to detect the risk of resignation.

105 www.pymetrics.com
106 Mickaël Cabrol, "L'intelligence artificielle, facteur de diversité dans le recrutement," Stratégies, 08/12/2017.
107 www.exclusiverh.com/articles/cvtheques/yatedo-mise-sur-l-intelligence-artificielle.htm

Internal Mobility

Through an Artificial Intelligence system, job descriptions are analyzed regarding candidate profiles for mobility. In a similar way to recruitment, using a math system, HR managers then identify the best candidates for a given position. It is quite possible that the AI may detect candidates for mobility, off the beaten track, whose profile, too far from the job definition, would have been rejected, while invisible gateways exist.

Company Case: L'Oréal Uses AI for its Recruitment

L'Oréal is already using AI to recruit in China, working with the Chinese startup Seedlink. In an interview108, Jean-Claude Legrand, Director of International Human Resources Development, explains that AI helps L'Oréal choose the best candidate, by screening profiles through the analysis of video questionnaires. Today, this tool is being tested in China and Argentina, and then deployed on a larger scale if the pilot is successful.

He cites the example of a Chinese employee who was originally a lawyer, without any knowledge of digital technology but who was selected by the AI and then chosen during the interview phase.

Now in her current position, she has achieved remarkable results in e-commerce. For Jean-Claude Legrand, this is the proof that we must increase efforts on augmented recruitment thanks to AI.

On the other hand, a similar experiment in Russia failed in May 2018 because it did not receive a positive response internally. This virtual HRD, called Vera, was responsible for screening profiles that could meet L'Oréal's needs and giving them a first telephone interview, using voice recognition.

"Innovation is at the heart of our recruitment strategy. To recruit the best and most diverse talent from all over the world, we are opening up our horizons to various initiatives and letting our subsidiaries initiate pilots who can become best practices throughout the group. Our Russian subsidiary was approached by Stafori, with whom there was a local experiment, in a spirit of Test and Learn,"

108 Jean-Claude Legrand, Director of International Human Resources Development at L'Oréal, interviewed for the #LinkedIn Top Companies ranking
https://lnkd.in/gxmjSNz

which was not conclusive," explains Natalia Noguera, head of digital transformation at L'Oréal.109

Onboarding

Hiring the best talent is not enough, it is important to welcome them and to onboard them so that they can quickly adapt to their new company. These newcomers require a lot of attention and time, and it is sometimes difficult to give it to them. That is where AI comes in. It determines a personalized reception process. This is extremely productive and increases the percentage of retention compared to their peers who have not benefited from this type of onboarding.

Training

Technological changes are forcing the pace of training. It is crucial for employees to continue to receive training on a permanent basis. AI can successfully plan, organize and coordinate training programs for all staff members, at an individual level if necessary. It can also offer personalized training courses.

AI will become a valuable assistant for training leaders and trainers. A recent Gartner study indicates that 90% of training professionals plan to increase or maintain their investment in Artificial Intelligence over the next two years.[110]

Assistant Trainer

The recognition of natural language, through text and voice, is one of the first victories of AI. It allows a more natural communication between humans and computers. These conversational interfaces (e. g. Chatbots) can be used in companies to allow employees to ask basic questions and get immediate answers from the AI system. It will always be available and will free up time for training departments and trainers to focus on more complex issues.

109 www.exclusiverh.com/articles/test-recrutement/l-oreal-limoge-son-robot-drh.htm
110 Gartner Learning Quarterly, q1, 2018.

Artificial Mentoring

Similarly, chatbots can be transformed into mentors to reinforce learning through tests, quizzes, etc., post-training.

For example, Duolingo offers learning Spanish, French or German at one's own pace and on one's own device.[111]

Content Production and Enrichment

The creation of training content is very time-consuming for business experts. AI can be trained to extract important information and put it in a format that can be read by employees in the form of e-learning. Thus, Content Technologies Inc's AI[112] uses book-based or article-based content to create training content, leaving more time for educators to enrich the user experience.

AI can also enrich existing training content, for example by adding links to a video or relevant article. This makes it possible to update training courses without wasting time.

Accessibility

AI can be a powerful ally in the search for and implementation of training accessibility. Microsoft has developed an application (Seeing AI) that explains to the visually impaired and blind what surrounds them.

This free application uses the smartphone's camera to identify objects and people in the user's environment. It is even able to recognize certain emotions. Seeing AI transmits orally to the smartphone owner what is around them. The objective: to provide them with enough detail to get a clearer picture of their environment.[113]

The same type of image recognition tools are already used on mainstream platforms such as Google photos, which identify people and objects. One could imagine that the AI would choose relevant illustrations for your e-learning from your favorite photo library.

On the website www.everypixel.com/aesthetics, you can see how

---

111 bots.duolingo.com/
112 contenttechnologiesinc.com/
113 "L'application de Microsoft qui parle aux aveugles," Les Échos, 16/07/2017.

an AI analyses pictures, classifies them by keywords, or even judges their aesthetic criteria!

Similarly, on video-based training, subtitles are an excellent way to make content accessible to all. YouTube uses its speech recognition technology to automatically create subtitles for your videos. These automatic subtitles are generated by machine learning algorithms, which explains why their quality may vary. Automatic subtitles are available for the following languages: German, English, Korean, Spanish, French, Italian, Japanese, Dutch, Portuguese and Russian.

Personalization

Personalization is probably the most visible way AI is used today. On the Internet, we are offered a lot of content thanks to this function. It is easy to imagine doing the same thing with the training content that could be offered to employees.

Imagine, for example, a sales consultant who wants to understand the specificities of a new product. They could connect to an Artificial Intelligence platform and search for this product. They are then offered several sub-themes including, for example, "Benefits for the client." By indicating the time available for training, they allow the AI to select relevant content (often in video format) and aggregate it into an interactive video training module.

This makes training more effective but also provides information on learner engagement and understanding.[114]

Employee Retention

Hiring talented employees is as difficult as retaining them. However, AI can analyze and anticipate the needs of staff members. It can determine individual affinities and propose targeted increases. It is also able to detect dissatisfaction versus the balance of professional/private life. A powerful ally for QWL[115] and in preventing talent attrition.

---

114 www.welcometothejungle.co/articles/intelligence-artificielle-revolutionner-formation-professional
115 Quality of Work Life.

Using AI platforms can give insight into what your employees are really looking for in their role and will allow you to draft behavior models. For example: employees who have not received salary increases for a long time, those who have work-life balance concerns, or those who feel pressured in the course of their work. This information can be correlated with what employees have chosen to share with their managers or HR, allowing them to act before the situation deteriorates.

Performance Analysis

AI allows for innovations in evaluation with the implementation of *ongoing* evaluation systems to respond to the increasingly frequent criticism of the famous annual interview, which is more of a cut-off point than a real motivation to perform.

Leadership Development

With AI platforms, managers can receive personalized messages and coaching to improve their leadership skills. They can also measure their managerial effectiveness by accessing dashboards that include information about the managerial effectiveness of their peers.

Career Management

Predictive algorithms provide career plans for employees. AI makes it possible to create a Career Roadmap, designed to help the employee in defining a medium- or long-term career plan to get as close as possible to their professional objectives.

For example, the Braincities[116] tool allows you to:
- analyze the personality of an asset;
- evaluate their technical skills and profile;
- support them in achieving their professional objectives, all within the framework of a personalized career plan.

Analysis of the Social Climate

---

116 www.braincities.co

The social climate analysis measures the degree of satisfaction of employees with their working environment. This analysis helps to better understand the link between employees and their company and to identify social risks. A favorable social climate contributes to a better performance of the organization and its monitoring is therefore strategic.

In this context, semantic analysis provides valuable information on the state of mind of employees. It opens up the field of possibilities to identify themes, opinions, evolutions, with various possibilities of focus (region, sector...)

How to proceed? Companies have a large amount of data from various and varied surveys. AI can quickly identify trends in the internal social climate.

AI-based solutions aggregate all survey responses and provide an automatic classification of the topics covered and their tonality.[117] Answers to closed-ended questions, departments and geographical areas are also taken into account to complete the analysis and suggest relevant data cross-referencing. The results are then refined with HR and priority areas for action are proposed.

This type of analysis can also focus on language, including tone of voice, and measure:

- the amount of stress or frustration in the voice of a customer or employee;
- how fast the individual speaks;
- changes in the level of stress in the person's discourse (for example, in response to a solution provided).

Payroll

In the field of payroll, the prospects around Artificial Intelligence focus mainly on the automation of often repetitive and time-consuming tasks. Software can be found on the market that automates the management of DSN[118] through analysis and recommendations for corrections or optimization.

117 Voie Revue Personnel n°568, March-April 2016.
118 *Déclaration Sociale Nominative*: Nominative Social Declaration

Answering Administrative Questions

Conversational robots (chatbots) appeal to large companies: they respond effectively, 24 hours a day, to their employees' HR questions.

Questions about the use of CPF[119], the number of days off, the annual interview, or even pension rights, are immediately answered by the chatbot, often from the company's intranet site

Example: The PSA Group (Peugeot Citroën) promotes self-service for its employees with a chatbot solution called Eva. Since 2012, the Digital Department has been implementing a self-service solution to meet the demands of its employees on questions related to helpdesks, HR and practical services, with the objective of providing an answer in less than 30 seconds and in less than 3 questions. This service is available in three languages (French, English and Spanish) to reach all employees and is accessible on the PSA Group's intranet portal.[120]

Challenges of the HR Department Using AI

Although promising, the use of AI by HR involves some challenges, particularly regarding the quality of the data collected.

Indeed, HR data is not always effectively managed by companies and is often collected and recorded in multiple locations, so applying an algorithm to a subset of data can lead to errors in the results.

The second challenge is the application of data usage rules. It is essential to explain to employees how their data will be used and based on which rules. Most employees accept that the company can access their personal data as long as the rules of use are clearly defined and applied.

The third challenge is that not everything in HR is black or white. There is never any certainty that a particular candidate is the best or

---

119 *Compte Personnel de Formation*: Personal Training Account.
120 www.doyoudreamup.com/blog/retour-dexperience-psa-peugeot-citroen

that a particular employee should be promoted. Almost all HR decisions require some judgment and subjectivity. Algorithms can therefore help to reduce this part of subjectivity, but this does not mean that they are 100% correct.

To conclude "don't equip yourself with a solution where you can't understand every part of the operation in detail!"[121]

---

121 Jérémy Lamri, Le Mag RH.

Chapter 7

Where to Start?

"I think we are coming to a pivotal period; companies can choose to transform themselves, whether technologically or humanly, to have a role to play in the future, or miss the opportunity to make the change and stay standing still."[122]

---

122 Stéphane Barberet, General Manager, Dell EMC France.

Preparing for the arrival of Artificial Intelligence is not a choice, it is an imperative. Where to start?

Whether at the company level, at the level of each AI project or at the level of the HR Department, the purpose of this chapter is to offer ideas for reflection and action. Preparing for the arrival of AI is possible at various scales.

Company Level: Acculturate and Give Meaning

The magnitude of the task can be impressive. The first logical step is to position your company in relation to its readiness and appetite for AI. For example, you can position it on this dial developed by the BCG.[123] The same exercise can be done at the level of each Directorate for a more detailed analysis.

In a second step, we recommend developing the acculturation of managers and executives to the theme of AI: to support the consideration of AI, its challenges and its impacts at all levels of the company.

It is also necessary to ensure that a calm climate is created and to build an ethical framework around these new technologies. The objective is to develop human-machine collaboration.

In parallel, it is necessary to give meaning to the deployment of AI by building a common vision with General Management and stakeholders (trades, IT, HR, social partners, wider eco-system), and to develop a communication/training program based on innovative and participatory pedagogical approaches.

In any case, it is important to give preference to pilot approaches and experiments highlighting the principle of "Test and Learn" to reduce reluctance.

Launching an internal work transformation lab allows employees to take control of the evolution of their position and their professional trajectory.

The implementation or reinforcement of processes and initiatives guarantees the proper use of data and algorithms (GDPR, algorithm

---

123 *"Intelligence Artificielle et Capital Humain, Quels défis pour les entreprises,"* BCG, March 2018.

quality audit, etc.).

AI Projects:
Integrating HRD from the
Reflection Phase

If your company is already in the pilot or deployment phase of an AI system, it is important to check that the following points are covered:

- Ensuring that all current and future AI projects include an impact analysis component covering human aspects (impacts on jobs, skills, workload, organization). This analysis should be done at the beginning of the project or iteratively in the case of an agile approach.
- Ensuring that business experts are involved in the construction of AI.
- Imposing HRD into the governance of all AI projects, and take the opportunity to preach the aspects of change management and occupational health.

HRD Level:
Being Proactive and Being a Pilot

Some HRDs are beginning to develop their own roadmap for deploying Artificial Intelligence within their department. There are realistic, simple and inexpensive application cases that you can already test to understand the contribution of AI to Human Resources management:

Training HR teams to understand the power of AI. It is about building AI expertise within your team. Designate a member of your team to be the point of contact with your CIO, Digital and

- Trade Transformation team and to feed the HR team with up-to-date information on new products and services, benchmarks on how other companies or internal departments such as marketing use AI to improve the customer/employee experience. The adoption of AI by companies is still low at this stage but there are many opportunities to develop a concrete and solid understanding of its eco-system and applications on HR processes. This first phase of acculturation will allow HR teams to take ownership of the cases of AI use within an HR department, in order to be piloted on the different processes: recruitment, performance, training, mobility.

- Engaging, from now on, in social dialogue on the subject of AI with social partners and involving them in the reflection as far in advance as possible.

- Starting a detailed impact analysis on jobs and skills, as well as on the working time potentially transferred to AI tools, trying to favor the *competencies* approach in relation to the *activity* approach.

- Controlling recruitment by identifying the skills needed to produce and deploy AI. Preparing the strategy for recruiting AI profiles.

- Adjusting the SWP site to include aspects related to the deployment of AI.

- Anticipating and preparing training and requalification efforts to support transformation. Developing synergies with a broader ecosystem (local fabric, university, region, startup...)

- Reviewing training processes and innovating by adopting a cognitive function approach. Do not hesitate to favor new training approaches (microlearning, gamification, experiential...).

- Equipping HRD with a chatbot.

Chatbots are already present in our lives as consumers, and they are beginning to appear in the workplace. Rather than just reading about this phenomenon, why not welcome a chatbot as a new member of the HR team? Why not implement a Test and Learn approach to deploying a chatbot to understand the power of AI on behavior change?

Chatbots are a new way of working by using natural language to plan meetings, generate documents and answer questions.

Thus, Orléans Métropole and the town hall of Orléans were the first local authorities in France to adopt a chatbot for agents to answer HR questions. The problem was simple, summarizes Karine Thilloux, HRD reception-orientation referent for the two communities, "many officers did not know where to go to get answers for their HR questions or as part of their administrative procedures." In total, the two entities have 3,500 employees, covering 200 different business lines and based on several geographical sites. The conversational agent, called O'RH, was set up in July 2017. It is available 7 days a week and 24 hours a day from the Internet, Intranet or by SMS.

"The chatbot has made it possible to offer all our agents a unique solution, available from anywhere and at any time of the day," says the referent. After six months of use, feedback from O'RH is positive. The chatbot handled an average of 200 questions per month.[124]

Identifying New Roles to Make the Best Use of AI in HR

Here is food for thought on possible new roles that will emerge within HR in the coming months or years.

Responsible for the Employee Experience

The concept of employee experience derives from the marketing concept of user experience. This takes into account the emotional aspects of the user's experience with a product, service, process or interface, with the objective of providing the best possible experience.

In the case of employee experience, this notion is applied to workers.

In practice, it is a question of considering the emotions and feelings of the employee in their relationship and interactions with their employer.

The employee experience therefore covers many aspects, such as the employment contract, hierarchical relationships, corporate culture, professional development and the nature of the assignments.

Responsible for the HR Conversational

124 www.cio-online.com/actualites/lire-orleans-lance-un-chatbot-rh-pour-ses-agents-10499.html

Experience

Recruitment becomes (anew) conversational and less transactional.

Who will write the chatbot conversations? Who will decide on the conversational path with the employee or candidate? What happens if the conversation fails? How to market the chatbot?

The person in charge of the HR conversational experience will be responsible, in particular, for deciding on the personality of the chatbot. This is what will make the experience different and memorable for the user. Unfortunately, chatbots are often created by developers and are boring (no matter what the developers think...). The conversation is effective but linear, without surprise or creativity. When the chatbot fails, they simply say "Sorry, I don't understand you" and the user feels frustrated.

Regarding ergonomics, the conversation designer must consider all the paths that the user could take to achieve their goal (for example: obtaining a telephone number, a list of positions related to their skills, etc.). Some users may need a lot of handholding, others may try to make the chatbot fail. The conversation is non-linear, so if you inject flexibility into your bot right from the design stage, it will be more engaging for the user. The richness of the scenarios considered will undoubtedly guarantee the satisfaction of your users.

HR Big Data Manager

The HR Big Data manager implements the HR data collection strategy (HRIS, career and recruitment site, employee evaluations, company statistics, social reports, etc.) and defines relevant indicators. It promotes the integration of systems to collect more data. It analyses the data collected to identify trends, variables and relationships that explain individual and collective performance. They work with AI teams to improve the predictive responses of algorithms.

Thank you for reading 'Augmented HR'.

If you enjoyed this book (or even if you didn't) please visit the site where you purchased it and write a brief review. Your feedback is important to me and will help other readers decide whether to read the book too.

Annex

A Few Movies and Series to Reflect on Artificial Intelligence

Movies

- *Metropolis*
Directed by Fritz Lang, Germany, 1927.

- *2001, A Space Odyssey*
Directed by Stanley Kubrick, United States/United Kingdom, 1968.

- *Blade Runner*
Directed by Ridley Scott, United States, 1982.

- *Tron*
Directed by Steven Lisberger, United States, 1982.

- *WarGames*
Directed by John Badham, United States, 1983.

- *Terminator*
Directed by James Cameron, United States, 1984.
The film had four sequences:
> *Terminator 2: The Last Judgment*, 1991;
> *Terminator 3: The Uprising of Machines*, 2003;
> *Terminator Renaissance*, 2009;
> *Terminator: Genisys*, 2015.

- *Matrix*
Directed by Andy and Larry Wachowski, United States/Australia, 1999. First part of the Matrix trilogy, which continues with *Matrix Reloaded* and *Matrix Revolutions*, 2003.

- *A.I. Artificial Intelligence*
Directed by Steven Spielberg, United States, 2001.

- *I, Robot*
Directed by Alex Proyas, United States, 2004.

- *Wall-E*
Directed by Andrew Stanton, United States, 2008.

- *Tron: The Legacy*
Directed by Joseph Kosinski, United States, 2010.

- *Eva*
Directed by Kike Maillo, Spain/France, 2011.

- *Robot & Frank*
Directed by Jake Schreier, United States, 2012.

- *Her*
Directed by Spike Jonze, United States, 2013.

- *Transcendence*
Directed by Wally Pfister, United States/United Kingdom/China, 2014.

- *Ex Machina*
Directed by Alex Garland, United Kingdom, 2015.

- *Chappie*
Directed by Neil Blomkamp, United States, 2015.

- *Imitation Game*
Directed by Morten Tyldum, United States, 2014.

- *Blade Runner 2049*
Directed by Denis Villeneuve, United States, 2017.

Series

- *Black Mirror*
United Kingdom, since 2011.

- *Real Humans*

Sweden, 2012-2014.

- *Mr Robot*

United States, since 2015.

- *Westworld*

United States, since 2016.

Glossary

Some Terms to Know When Talking About HR and Artificial Intelligence

Algorithm
Description of a finite and unambiguous sequence of steps or instructions to obtain a result from input elements.

API
Application Programming Interface. Interface allowing the provision and exchange of data.

Apprenance
French neologism that defines an individual and collective attitude and practices. It is the will to stay in tune with one's ecosystem. It expresses a willingness to learn and to learn together at four levels: individual, organizational, inter-organizational and societal. This is the approach used by learning organizations. Finally, *apprenance* is different from learning, which has a more individual, sometimes more contractual dimension, from the *master* to the *student*. However, *apprenance* and learning are two complementary attitudes.

Artificial Neural Network
A system whose design is originally schematically inspired by the functioning of biological neurons, and which has subsequently moved closer to statistical methods. Because they are very flexible, they represent models that are not as subject to bias.

Big Data
Refers to the conjunction between, on the one hand, huge volumes of data that have become difficult to process in the digital age and, on the other hand, the new techniques for processing these data and drawing correlations.

Chatbot or Conversational Bot
Conversational agent capable of simulating a conversation, performing a task or providing advice, with one or more humans by voice or text exchange. In their operation, the bots follow the rules designed by their developers and display pre-recorded responses.

CNIL
Commission Nationale de l'Informatique et des Libertés.

Cobot
Collaborative Robot.

Cognitive Agent
Software that acts autonomously and intelligently.

CSR
Corporate Social Responsibility.

Cognitive Science
Multidisciplinary field of research on mechanisms and the functioning of mental processes. Cognitive science seeks to describe the mechanisms of human thought, consciousness and intelligence, in part with the aim of reproducing them in computer systems. This science includes several disciplines such as psychology, linguistics,

neuroscience or computer science.

CPF
Compte Personnel de Formation (Personal Training Account.)

Data Base
Collection of works, data or other independent elements, arranged in a systematic or methodical manner, and individually accessible by electronics or any other means in accordance with Article L. 112-3 of the Intellectual Property Code.

Deep Learning
Machine learning method that is part of the Artificial Intelligence research field. Deep learning allows unsupervised learning. It is based on the analysis of a data model. It is particularly suitable for image recognition or natural language processing.

Expert System
Software that reproduces the cognitive mechanisms of an expert in a specialized field. It is able to answer questions by making reasoning based on known facts and rules. It can be used as a decision-making tool.

GAFA
The term GAFA, which appeared in the mid-2000s, is an acronym formed by the initial letter of the four companies: Google, Apple, Facebook and Amazon. There is also sometimes the acronym GAFAM for Google, Apple, Facebook, Amazon and Microsoft. This acronym refers to global Internet players.

GDPR
General Data Protection Regulations.

SWP (GPEC)
Gestion Prévisionnelle des Emplois et des Compétences, or strategic workforce planning. It is the anticipation and planning of the company's strategy, and the evaluation of skills necessary to carry out the business plan.

HMI or Human Machine Interface
Any interface allowing information to be transmitted between an individual and a digital device unilaterally or interactively. There are input and output HMIs, allowing data acquisition and restitution respectively. Common examples of input HMIs include: mouse, keyboard, sensor, touch screen, microphone, camera... Common examples of output HMIs include: screen, printer, loudspeaker...

Machine Learning (or Automatic Learning)
A branch of Artificial Intelligence, based on methods of learning and automatic acquisition of new knowledge by computers, which allows them to act without having to be explicitly programed.

MOOC
Massive Online Open Course. Training provided on the Internet and accessible to the public. This type of course offers everyone the opportunity to evaluate their knowledge and can lead to a certification (sometimes for a fee).

NLP
Natural Language Processing. A very important branch of machine learning and therefore of Artificial Intelligence. NLP is a program's ability to understand human language.

Personal Data
Any information relating to an identified natural person or that can be identified, directly or indirectly, by reference to an identification number or to one or more elements specific to it according to Article 2 of the Data Protection Act.

Predictability

The nature of what is predictable, what can be anticipated.

Predictive Analysis

Predictive analysis, considered a type of data mining, is a field of statistical analysis that extracts information from the data to predict future trends and patterns of behavior.

Reverse Mentoring

A new principle introduced by large groups, which consists in assigning experienced managers a mentor who is none other than a millennial (Gen Y) employee.

RPA

Robotic Process Automation

Supervised Machine Learning

The algorithm learns from inputted data qualified by humans and thus defines rules based on examples that are validated cases.

Test and Learn

Test and Learn is a method of testing an idea or process on a small scale, learning from it and thus making improvements, before generalizing the test.

Turing Test

Proposed by the British mathematician Alan Turing in 1950, it is intended to evaluate the intelligence of a machine or system by testing its ability to conduct a conversation in natural language. A human operator faces another human and a machine anonymously; they must determine, through textual exchanges, which of their interlocutors is the machine.

Unsupervised Machine Learning

The algorithm learns from raw data and develops its own classification, which is free to evolve to any end state when a pattern or element is presented to it. A practice that requires instructors to teach the machine how to learn.

Bibliography

Books

ABERKANE I., *Libérez votre cerveau !* Robert Laffont, 2016.

ALEXANDRE L., *La Guerre des intelligences*, JC Lattes, 2017.

BARABEL m., Lamri J., *Innovations RH – Passer en mode digital et agile*, Dunod, 2017.

BOUZOU N., *Le travail est l'avenir de l'homme*, Édition L'Observatoire, 2017.

BRYNJOLFSSON E., MCAFEE A. *Le Deuxième âge de la machine, Travail et prospérité à l'heure de la révolution technologique*, Éditions Odile Jacob, 2015.

DAUGHERTY P. R., WILSON H. J., *Human + Machine, Reimagining work at the age of IA*, HBR Review Press, 2018.

DEVILLERS L., *Des Robots et des Hommes*, Plon, 2017.

DUMOUCHEL P., DAMIANO L., *Vivre avec les robots, Essai sur l'empathie artificielle*, Le Seuil, 2016.

GANASCIA J.-G., *Intelligence artificielle – vers une domination programmée ?*, 2nd edition, Le Cavalier Bleu, 2017.

HARARI Y. N., DAUZAT P.-E., *Sapiens, une brève histoire de l'humanité*, Albin Michel, 2015.

MALLARD S., Disruption, Dunod, 2018.

Reports and Studies

ACCENTURE, "Future Workforce Worker and C-Suite Surveys," 2017.
https://www.accenture.com/t20180418T033232Z__w__/us-en/_acnmedia/Accenture/Conversion-Assets/DotCom/DotCom/Documents/Global/PDF/About-Accenture/Accenture-AI-Future-Workforce-Insurance-Transcript.pdf

ARNTZ M., GREGORY T., ZIERAHN U., "The Risk of Automation for Jobs in OECD Countries," OCDE, May 2016.
https://www.zew.de/en/publikationen/the-risk-of-automation-for-jobs-in-oecd-countries-a-comparative-analysis/

ATHLING, "L'Intelligence Artificielle dans la Banques, Emplois et Compétence," December 2017.

http://www.observatoire-metiers-banque.fr/mediaServe/Etude_IA_emploi_compétences.pdf?ixh=374188114747685077070

ATKINSON R., WU J., "False Alarmism: Technological Disruption and the US Labor Market,1850-2015", ITIF, 2017.
http://www2.itif.org/2017-false-alarmism-technological-disruption.pdf

BOSTON CONSULTING GROUP & MALAKOFF MEDERIC, "*Intelligence Artificielle et Capital Humain,*" March 2018.
https://media-publications.bcg.com/Intelligence-artificielle-et-capital-human.pdf

VILLANI C., "*Donner un sens à l'intelligence Artificielle. Pour une stratégie nationale et européenne,*" March 2018.
http://www.ladocumentationfrancaise.fr/rapports-publics/184000159/index.shtml

CONSEIL D'ORIENTATION POUR L'EMPLOI, "*Automatisation, numérisation et emploi,*" September 2017.
http://www.coe.gouv.fr/Synthese_Report_Automatisation_numerisation_et_emploi_Tome_2a993.pdf

CNIL, "*Comment permettre à l'Homme de garder la main ? Rapport sur les enjeux éthiques des algorithmes et de l'intelligence artificielle,*" 15/12/2017.
https://www.cnil.fr/fr/comment-permettre-lhomme-de-garder-la-main-rapport-sur-les-enjeux-ethiques-des-algorithmes-et-de

CNIL, "*Règlement européen de protection des données.*"
www.cnil.fr/fr/reglement-europeen-protection-donnees

GARTNER, "Gartner Reports First Quarter 2018," May 2018.
https://investor.gartner.com/press-releases/press-release-details/2018/
Gartner-Reports-First-Quarter-2018-Financial-Results/default.aspx

GREGORY T., SALOMONS A., ZIERAHN U., "Racing With or Against the Machine? Evidence from Europe", July 2016.
http://ftp.zew.de/pub/zew-docs/dp/dp16053.pdf

INRIA, "*Intelligence artificielle, les défis actuels et l'action d'Inria*"
https://www.inria.fr/actualite/actualites-inria/intelligence-artificielle-les-defis-actuels-et-l-action-d-inria

KPMG International, "2018 Gobal CEO Outlook."

MCKINSEY, "An Executive's Guide to AI".
https://www.mckinsey.com/business-functions/mckinsey-analytics/our-insights/an-executives-guide-to-ai

MCKINSEY, "Jobs lost, jobs gained: What the future of work will mean for jobs, skills and wages", November 2017.
https://www.mckinsey.com/global-themes/future-of-organizations-and-

work/what-the-future-of-work-will-mean-for-jobs-skills-and- wages#part%201

MCKINSEY, "Where Machines Could Replace Humans – and Where They Can't (Yet)", July 2016.
https://www.mckinsey.com/business-functions/digital-mckinsey/our-insights/where-machines-could-replace-humans-and-where-they-cant-yet –

ZACKLAD M., Intelligence Artificielle :représentations et impacts sociétaux, CNAM, 2017.

Articles

Atelier BPN Paribas, *"L'avenir de l'assistant virtuel : vers une intelligence artificielle omnisciente ?,"* March 2016.
https://atelier.bnpparibas/life-work/article/enquete-l-avenir-assistant-virtuel- artificial-intelligence-omniscient

BYS C., *"La bonne acceptation de l'IA est une affaire de DRH, pas de DSI, assure Sylvain Duranton (BCG),"* Usine nouvelle, 23/03/2018.
https://www.usinenouvelle.com/article/la-bonne-integration-et-acceptation-de-l-ia-is-a-a-drh-pas-de-dsi-assure-sylvain-duranton-bcg.N670674

CABROL M., *"Intelligence artificielle et recrutement : l'ère de la diversité,"* La Tribune, 20/12/2017.
https://www.latribune.fr/opinions/tribunes/intelligence-artificielle-et-recrute-ment-l-ere-de-la-diversite-762178.html

CABROL M., *"L'intelligence artificielle, facteur de diversité dans le recrutement,"* Stratégies, 08/12/2017.
http://www.strategies.fr/blogs-opinions/idees-tribunes/4003538W/l-intelligence-artificielle-facteur-de-diversite-in-the-recruitment.html

CARUSO, C., "Time to Fold, Humans: Poker-Playing AI Beats Pros at Texas Hold'em," Scientific American, 02/03/2017.
https://www.scientificamerican.com/article/time-to-fold-humans-poker-playing-ai-beats-pros-at-texas-hold-rsquo-em/

Élysée.fr *"Transcription du discours du Président de la République, Emmanuel Macron, sur l'intelligence artificielle,"* 04/04/2018.
http://www.elysee.fr/declarations/article/transcription-du-discours-du-pres-ident-de-la-republique-emmanuel-macron-on-artificial-intelligence/

FAGUER L., *"L'intelligence artificielle s'invite avec justesse chez Kiehl's,"* Frenchweb, 20/08/2048.
https://www.frenchweb.fr/lintelligence-artificielle-sinvite-avec-justesse-chez-kiehls/320176

GARREAU M., *"Se former face à l'intelligence artificielle et la robotique, oui, mais comment ?"* Usine nouvelle, 26/09/2017.
https://www.usinenouvelle.com/editorial/se-former-face-a-l-intelligence-

GEORGES B, *"Le travail ne meurt pas, il se transforme,"* Les Échos , 15/09/2017.
https://www.lesechos.fr/2017/09/le-travail-ne-meurt-pas-il-se-transforme-181863#ujuHyZKs1FJKLcr1.99lutôt

GRONDIN A., "France Aprenante, une coalition pour transformer la formation en profondeur," Les Echos, 17/05/2018.
https://business.lesechos.fr/entrepreneurs/idees-de-business/0301684784534-france-apprenante-une-coalition-pour-transformer-la-formation-en-profondeur-320973.php

GUYONNET P., *"La reconnaissance faciale de l'IPhone X peut servir à essayer des lunettes,"* Huffington Post, 08/11/2017.
https://www.huffingtonpost.fr/2017/11/08/la-reconnaissance-faciale-de-liphone-x-peut-servir-a-essayer-des-lunettes_a_23271061/?utm_hp_ref=fr-reconnaissance-faciale

HENNO J., *"1968 : avec Kubrick, l'IA devient star de cinéma,"* Les Échos, 23/08/2017.
https://www.lesechos.fr/idees-debats/sciences-prospective/030505454511-1968-with-kubrick-lia-devient-star-de-cinema-2109167.php

HEUDIN J.-C., *"Les trois lois d'Asimov sont-elles utiles ?"* Futura Tech, 09/01/2016.
https://www.futura-sciences.com/tech/dossiers/robotique-trois-lois-robo-tique-1836/page/4/

JESUTHASAN R., BOUDREAU J., "Thinking through how automation will affect your workforce", Harvard Business Review, 20/04/2017.
https://hbr.org/2017/04/thinking-through-how-automation-will-affect-your-workforce

KOCH C., "How the Computer Beat the Go Master", Scientific American, 19/03/2016.
https://www.scientificamerican.com/article/how-the-computer-beat-the-go-master/

LAMRI J., *"Le numérique expliqué aux DRH,"* Forbes, 03/10/2017.
https://www.forbes.fr/business/le-numerique-explique-aux-drh/

LELIEVRE A., "Le Crédit Mutuel accélère dans l'intelligence artificielle," Les Échos, 20/04/2017.
https://www.lesechos.fr/20/04/2017/lesechos.fr/0211991417503_le-credit-mutuel-accelere- danss-intelligence-artificielle.htm

LELIEVRE A., *"Samsung va créer un centre de recherche dédié à l'IA en France,"* Les Échos, 28/03/2018.
https://www.lesechos.fr/tech-medias/hightech/0301497193692-samsung-et-fujitsu-vont-creer-des-centers-de-research-dedies-a-lia-en-france-2164999.php

RAMDANI M., *"Chez Salesforce : une IA au comité de direction !"* LinkedIn Pulse, 26/01/2018.
https://fr.linkedin.com/pulse/chez-salesforce-une-ia-au-comit%C3%A9-de-direction-mehdi-ramdani

ROLLAND S., *"Hub France IA : la filière de l'intelligence artificielle n'attend pas l'État pour se mobiliser,"* La Tribune, 21/12/2017.
https://www.latribune.fr/technos-medias/hub-france-ia-la-filiere-de-l-intelligence-artificielle-n-attend-pas-l-etat-pour-se-mobiliser-762487.html

RONFAUT L., "Facebook investit 10 millions dans l'intelligence artificielle en France," Le Figaro, 22/01/2018.
http://www.lefigaro.fr/secteur/high-tech/2018/01/22/32001-20180122ARTFIG0000008-facebook-investit-10-millions-ins-l-intelligence-artificielle-en-france.php

ROZIÈRES G., *"L'intelligence artificielle de Google gagne 4 à 1 au jeu de go face au champion du monde Lee Sedol,"* Huffington Post, 05/10/2016.
http://www.huffingtonpost.fr/2016/03/15/google-jeu-de-go-intelligence-artificial-deep-mind-lee-sedol_n_9466926.html

ROZIÈRES G., *"Une intelligence artificielle vient de battre quatre champions de poker (on s'y attendait, mais pas si tôt),"* Huffington Post, 31/01/2017.
http://www.huffingtonpost.fr/2017/01/31/une-intelligence-artificielle-vient-de-battre-quatre-champions-d_a_21703279/

TACHOT A., *"L'Oréal limoge son robot DRH,"* Exclusive RH, 11/05/2018.
https://www.exclusiverh.com/articles/test-recrutement/l-oreal-limoge-son-robot-drh.htm

WAJSBROT S. LEDERER E. *"Formation : les banques face au défi des métiers de demain,"* Les Échos, 06/07/2018.
https://www.lesechos.fr/finance-marches/banque-assurances/0301930970825-Training-the-banks-face-at-the-defield-of-tomorrow's-jobs-2190134.php

WORLD ECONOMIC FORUM, "The future of education, according to experts at Davos," 26/01/2018.
https://www.weforum.org/agenda/2018/01/top-quotes-from-davos-on-the-future-of-education/

"L'application de Microsoft qui parle aux aveugles," Les Échos, 16/07/2017.
https://www.lesechos.fr/16/07/2017/lesechos.fr/030446614645_l-applica-tion-de-microsoft-qui parle-aux-aux-a blind.htm

Printed in Poland
by Amazon Fulfillment
Poland Sp. z o.o., Wrocław

52585601R00052